T0194658

MACAT

An Analysis of

# Eric Hoffer

## The True Believer
### Thoughts on the Nature of Mass Movements

Jonah S. Rubin

Published by Macat International Ltd
24:13 Coda Centre, 189 Munster Road, London SW6 6AW.

Distributed exclusively by Routledge
2 Park Square, Milton Park, Abingdon, Oxon OX14 4RN
711 Third Avenue, New York, NY 10017, USA

*Routledge is an imprint of the Taylor & Francis Group, an informa business*

www.macat.com
info@macat.com

*Cataloguing in Publication Data*
A catalogue record for this book is available from the British Library.
Library of Congress Cataloguing-in-Publication Data is available upon request.
Cover illustration: A. Richard Allen

ISBN 978-1-912303-60-1 (hardback)
ISBN 978-1-912128-14-3 (paperback)
ISBN 978-1-912282-48-7 (e-book)

**Notice**
The information in this book is designed to orientate readers of the work under analysis,
to elucidate and contextualise its key ideas and themes, and to aid in the development
of critical thinking skills. It is not meant to be used, nor should it be used, as a
substitute for original thinking or in place of original writing or research. References and
notes are provided for informational purposes and their presence does not constitute
endorsement of the information or opinions therein. This book is presented solely for
educational purposes. It is sold on the understanding that the publisher is not engaged
to provide any scholarly advice. The publisher has made every effort to ensure that
this book is accurate and up-to-date, but makes no warranties or representations with
regard to the completeness or reliability of the information it contains. The information
and the opinions provided herein are not guaranteed or warranted to produce particular
results and may not be suitable for students of every ability. The publisher shall not be
liable for any loss, damage or disruption arising from any errors or omissions, or from
the use of this book, including, but not limited to, special, incidental, consequential or
other damages caused, or alleged to have been caused, directly or indirectly, by the
information contained within.

# CONTENTS

# THE MACAT LIBRARY

The Macat Library is a series of unique academic explorations of seminal works in the humanities and social sciences – books and papers that have had a significant and widely recognised impact on their disciplines. It has been created to serve as much more than just a summary of what lies between the covers of a great book. It illuminates and explores the influences on, ideas of, and impact of that book. Our goal is to offer a learning resource that encourages critical thinking and fosters a better, deeper understanding of important ideas.

Each publication is divided into three Sections: Influences, Ideas, and Impact. Each Section has four Modules. These explore every important facet of the work, and the responses to it.

This Section-Module structure makes a Macat Library book easy to use, but it has another important feature. Because each Macat book is written to the same format, it is possible (and encouraged!) to cross-reference multiple Macat books along the same lines of inquiry or research. This allows the reader to open up interesting interdisciplinary pathways.

To further aid your reading, lists of glossary terms and people mentioned are included at the end of this book (these are indicated by an asterisk [*] throughout) – as well as a list of works cited.

Macat has worked with the University of Cambridge to identify the elements of critical thinking and understand the ways in which six different skills combine to enable effective thinking.
Three allow us to fully understand a problem; three more give us the tools to solve it. Together, these six skills make up the **PACIER** model of critical thinking. They are:

**ANALYSIS** – understanding how an argument is built
**EVALUATION** – exploring the strengths and weaknesses of an argument
**INTERPRETATION** – understanding issues of meaning

**CREATIVE THINKING** – coming up with new ideas and fresh connections
**PROBLEM-SOLVING** – producing strong solutions
**REASONING** – creating strong arguments

To find out more, visit **WWW.MACAT.COM.**

# CRITICAL THINKING AND *THE TRUE BELIEVER*

## Primary critical thinking skill: CREATIVE THINKING
## Secondary critical thinking skill: ANALYSIS

Eric Hoffer's *The True Believer: Thoughts on the Nature of Mass Movements* is one of the most widely read works of social psychology written in the 20th-century. It exemplifies the powers of creative thinking and critical analysis at their best, providing an insight into two crucial elements of critical thinking.

Hoffer is likely to go down in history as one of America's great creative thinkers – a writer not bound by standard frameworks of thinking or academic conventions, willing to beat his own path in framing the best possible answers to the questions he investigated. An impoverished, largely unschooled manual laborer who had survived the worst effects of the Great Depression in the United States, Hoffer was a passionate autodidact whose philosophical and psychological education came from omnivorous reading. Working without the help of any mentors, he forged the fearsomely creative and individual approach to problems demonstrated in *The True Believer*.

The book, which earned him his reputation, examines the different phenomena of fanaticism – religious or political – and applies Hoffer's analytical skills to reveal that, deep down, all 'true believers' display the same needs and tendencies, whatever their final choice of belief. Incisive and persuasive, it remains a classic.

## ABOUT THE AUTHOR OF THE ORIGINAL WORK

We know little about **Eric Hoffer's** early life. The story he himself told—that he was born in New York City in 1902, to working-class German immigrants who died when he was young—has never been verified. His biographer suspects Hoffer was himself a German immigrant, born in 1898, who entered the US illegally from Mexico. Despite never receiving a formal education, Hoffer read voraciously. He spent his entire working life as a longshoreman on the docks in San Francisco. When *The True Believer*, his most famous work, was published in 1951, the "Longshoreman-Philosopher" became a media sensation. Hoffer went on to be awarded the Presidential Medal of Freedom just a few short months before his death in 1983.

## ABOUT THE AUTHORS OF THE ANALYSIS

**Dr. Jonah S. Rubin** holds a PhD in anthropology from the University of Chicago, focusing on memory and death in post-Franco Spain. He is currently a visiting professor in anthropology at Bard College, New York

## ABOUT MACAT

### GREAT WORKS FOR CRITICAL THINKING

Macat is focused on making the ideas of the world's great thinkers accessible and comprehensible to everybody, everywhere, in ways that promote the development of enhanced critical thinking skills.

It works with leading academics from the world's top universities to produce new analyses that focus on the ideas and the impact of the most influential works ever written across a wide variety of academic disciplines. Each of the works that sit at the heart of its growing library is an enduring example of great thinking. But by setting them in context – and looking at the influences that shaped their authors, as well as the responses they provoked – Macat encourages readers to look at these classics and game-changers with fresh eyes. Readers learn to think, engage and challenge their ideas, rather than simply accepting them.

# WAYS IN TO THE TEXT

## KEY POINTS

- Eric Hoffer (1898–1983) was a self-educated longshoreman working on the docks, who lived in San Francisco in the United States. He wrote in his spare time.

- Hoffer's unique approach in *The True Believer* was to look at radical political movements and dissect their psychological appeal to frustrated individuals, rather than simply analyze their stated beliefs.

- Published in 1951, *The True Believer* was one of the most popular academic works of the 1950s and 1960s. The book received renewed interest following the terrorist attacks on the United States of September 11, 2001,* as modern scholars try to explain why some people volunteer to die in the name of political or religious ideas.

### Who was Eric Hoffer?

Born in New York City in the United States in 1898, Eric Hoffer was a self-educated laborer who wrote philosophical, psychological, and literary works in his spare time. He moved to California as a young man in search of work, after both his parents died. While he never received a formal education, Hoffer was nevertheless a passionate reader. He moved around frequently looking for a stable job, but wherever he went, Hoffer always rented a modest room near the municipal library. After being exempted from the mandatory draft during World War II\* because of a hernia, Hoffer found a job as a longshoreman on the San Francisco docks. In the late 1940s, as he started to think deeply about the postwar world, he began writing his first book, *The True Believer: Thoughts on the Nature of Mass Movements*.

Partly due to Hoffer's incredible life story, the book became an overnight success and remained popular throughout the following two decades. By 1967 it had sold over 500,000 copies. After its publication, Hoffer became an in-demand public intellectual and was interviewed on national television, as well as being appointed to a US presidential commission—a group of people put together at the request of the president to undertake a specific task of research or investigation—by Lyndon B. Johnson.\* The University of California, Berkeley hired Hoffer as an adjunct professor in the late 1950s and he rose to the position of senior research professor. Yet Hoffer continued to work on the docks until union rules forced him to retire at the age of 67.

In 1983, President Ronald Reagan\* awarded Hoffer the Presidential Medal of Freedom,\* America's highest civilian honor, calling him "an example of both the opportunity and the vitality of the American way of life."[1] Hoffer died in his modest home in San Francisco in 1983, at the age of 84.

## What Does *The True Believer* Say?

In *The True Believer: Thoughts on the Nature of Mass Movements*, Eric Hoffer argues that mass movements\*—the radical politicization of urban populations—have many similar features. Regardless of the specific political, religious, or ideological beliefs of the particular people involved, mass movements all appeal to the same type of individual. Hoffer spends the majority of the book describing the psychological profile of those who join these extremist groups. He also details the types of leaders they attract and how these movements develop.

Most analysts study extremist organizations by analyzing the words and writings of their leaders. First, they try to understand the group's philosophy, their ideas. Then they look to describe why a specific group of people finds this ideology so attractive. But Hoffer takes a different approach. He argues that the people who join cults,* fascist* and authoritarian* parties, or political movements all suffer from the same psychological shortcomings. These individuals have low self-esteem,* finding little of worth in their own characters. They have become frustrated with their own situations, have lost all faith in themselves, and, as a result, no longer value their individual identity.

According to Hoffer, mass movements step in to fill this void in the frustrated individual: "Faith [in the extremist group] in a holy cause is to a considerable extent a substitute for the lost faith in ourselves."[2] Extremist organizations replace people's lost sense of self-worth with a focus on the group. Since the people these groups appeal to already want to change their lives, they are willing to abandon their individuality and devote themselves to an organization that promises to radically alter the world. Followers profess undying loyalty to the group's leaders and show unquestioning faith in its mission and, having abandoned any sense of personal self-worth, they become willing to die for the cause.

Since the types of people who join mass movements all have the same characteristics, Hoffer argues, extremist groups are interchangeable. People join mass movements to escape their own frustrations and to find a sense of purpose. Yet, the specific group they join is really a coincidence, rather than being about a specific ideology. In fact, Hoffer claims that people who manage to escape one mass movement often end up joining another. This happens because they have not resolved the underlying psychological sense of inferiority that led them to join such a group in the first place. Since mass movements recruit from the same population, this also means that extremist groups compete directly with one another for recruits.

When a person joins a mass movement, he or she is no longer available for recruitment by another. One mass movement's gain is another extremist group's loss.

Hoffer wrote *The True Believer* after witnessing the fascism of Nazi* Germany and the rising totalitarianism* of Soviet* Russia beginning to regulate all aspects of their citizens' lives. However, Hoffer did not believe that mass movements are always evil. At times, he argues, a mass movement can be a necessary source of good, of renewal and revival. He sees India's pioneer of nonviolent resistance Mohandas Karmachand "Mahatma" Gandhi* and US presidents Abraham Lincoln* and Franklin Delano Roosevelt* as leaders of positive mass movements.

### Why Does *The True Believer* Matter?

Hoffer's work inspired academics and politicians who wanted to understand movements that appealed to regular people, or populist movements.* *The True Believer* persuaded Americans to look at mass movements not only by examining the speeches and slogans of their leaders, but also by looking at the social and psychological conditions of their members.

Hoffer originally wrote the book after thinking about both Nazism and Stalinism.* At the time, most analysts saw these two movements as polar opposites. After all, they had been on opposite sides of the battlefield during World War II as Germany opposed Russia. Hoffer wanted his work to explain the appeal of both movements using a single framework. This novel yet understandable approach made it an instant success, with American politicians praising the book's emphasis on individuality and self-reliance as an antidote to the allure of mass movements. Hoffer's storybook biography, which exemplified the American dream* that hard work and honesty will see you do well out of life, also inspired people to read it. *The True Believer* had a major impact on sociologists studying radical political movements, especially those interested in how fringe social groups develop over time and eventually gain mainstream acceptance. Hoffer's work provides a model for studying the role of individual believers in forming the nucleus of a mass movement.

But perhaps the greatest testament to *The True Believer* is the durability of its ideas. Following the terrorist attacks by Islamic fundamentalist\* group al-Qaeda\* on the United States on September 11, 2001, many commentators wondered why individuals would willingly volunteer to kill themselves in the name of religion. Publishers rushed *The True Believer* back into print, because its arguments about how people lose their sense of self and become willing to die for a cause seemed more relevant than ever. Drawing on Hoffer's work, modern writers look to understand the psychological factors that lead people to join radical militant groups. Today, analysts often talk about how terrorist organizations take advantage of poverty and frustration to breed hatred and radicalism. *The True Believer* provides a language for understanding how these social and psychological conditions might well create a fertile ground for radical groups.

Over six decades after its publication, *The True Believer* is still essential reading for anyone interested in political mobilization. The work provides a good insight into transnational terrorist organizations, populist political movements, religious revivals, and political trends. It is clear that Eric Hoffer's thinking and ideas have stretched way beyond his own lifetime.

## NOTES

1 Ronald Reagan, "Remarks at the Presentation Ceremony for the Presidential Medal of Freedom," Reagan Presidential Library, February 23, 1983, accessed October 22, 2015, http://www.reagan.utexas.edu/archives/ speeches/1983/22383c.htm.

2 Eric Hoffer, *The True Believer: Thoughts on the Nature of Mass Movements* (New York: Harper & Row, 1951), 14.

# SECTION 1
# INFLUENCES

# MODULE 1
# THE AUTHOR AND THE HISTORICAL CONTEXT

## KEY POINTS

- In writing *The True Believer*, Eric Hoffer made a major contribution to our understanding of radical political and religious movements.

- A self-educated longshoreman working on the docks, Hoffer wrote this text based on his experiences living through World War II.*

- Hoffer wrote *The True Believer* as scholars and politicians around the world debated about how to relate to the communist* Soviet Union* in the new world that was being fashioned in the aftermath of World War II.

### Why Read This Text?

In his 1951 bestseller, *The True Believer: Thoughts on the Nature of Mass Movements*, Eric Hoffer describes the kind of individuals who are susceptible to joining extremist organizations. Hoffer argues that it is not the ideas professed by such mass movements* that attract these individuals. Instead, he says these people act out of a sense of desperation and hopelessness. Having lost all sense of self-worth, they become willing to cast their lot in with a particular group and follow its leaders blindly. Arguing that the causes of all mass movements are psychological (arising in the mind and out of a person's mental state), Hoffer argues that extremist groups have many traits in common. Regardless of their religious, political, or ideological standpoint, these organizations all draw their supporters from the same pool of frustrated individuals.

❝ Eric Hoffer is a pink-faced, horny-handed San Francisco dock worker who pays his dues to Harry Bridges' longshoremen's union and preaches self-reliance more stalwartly than Emerson. He gets up at 4:45 in the morning and spends his days working on the piers of San Francisco's Embarcadero. Evenings he spends in his room in a shabby McAllister Street lodging house, bent over a plank desk writing. ❞

*Time*, "Dockside Montaigne"

Reportedly one of US president Dwight D. Eisenhower's* favorite books, *The True Believer* became one of the most popular works of the 1950s and 1960s. It had a major impact on sociologists studying organizational culture and political movements. Hoffer analyzed the role diehards play in forming the backbone of any radical social movement. In doing so, he shed light on how a small group of individuals can effect large-scale change.

Although the book slowly fell out of fashion in the second half of the twentieth century, it has recently enjoyed a popular revival. Following the terrorist attacks on the United States by Islamist fundamentalist group al-Qaeda* on September 11, 2001,* both scholars and media personalities returned to Hoffer's key text. In it, they found a language to describe why someone might choose to end his or her life of their own accord and in the name of religion. Drawing on Hoffer's work, these analysts explained groups like al-Qaeda and ISIS* not by analyzing the ideas found in terrorist leaders' speeches and writings; instead, they looked at how political and economic failings produce large numbers of frustrated, hopeless individuals. Seeing little possibility of real change in their own lives, they become willing to give them up for a cause.

### Author's Life

Despite his fame as a public intellectual, we know remarkably little about Eric Hoffer's early life.

In interviews, Hoffer claimed to have been born in 1902 to working-class German immigrants in New York City. At the age of seven, his mother tumbled down the stairs while carrying him in her arms. The accident killed his mother and left Hoffer blind for the next seven years: "When my eyesight came back, I was seized with an enormous hunger for the printed word. I read indiscriminately everything within reach—English and German."[1] After the death of his father in 1920, Hoffer moved to California.

For a number of reasons, biographers have cast doubt on much of Hoffer's account. They have not located any records for either of his parents in New York City. No childhood acquaintances ever emerged, even after Hoffer became a public figure. Ophthalmologists who specialize in studying the eye have also called Hoffer's account of losing his eyesight improbable. His biographer Tom Bethell* speculates that Hoffer was born in 1898, and was in fact a German who migrated illegally across the Mexican border looking for work.[2]

Regardless of how Hoffer got to California, however, records confirm that he worked for 10 years in the state as a farmhand, day laborer, and gold miner around Nevada City, eventually becoming a longshoreman working on the docks in San Francisco. Despite having no formal education to speak of, Hoffer read avidly. With the stability granted by his work on the San Francisco docks, he began polishing his writing. *The True Believer* became his first significant publication in 1951.

### Author's Background

In *The True Believer*, Eric Hoffer explains why certain people give up their sense of individuality to join radical social movements. His experiences during and after World War II heavily influenced his interest in this particular topic. Hoffer was especially concerned by Nazi* Germany's success in recruiting vast numbers of willing volunteers, despite the Nazi party's overt racism, and by the totalitarian* tendencies of Stalinist* Russia exemplified by the denial of individual liberty.

Soon after the 1951 publication of *The True Believer*, two mass movements took hold in the United States, most notably the Civil Rights Movement* (demanding an end to legal discrimination against African Americans) and the anti-Vietnam War* movement (demanding that the US withdraw from the war it waged in Vietnam from 1964 to 1975). The same concerns that motivated Hoffer to write *The True Believer* also led him to be very skeptical of both movements. He accused these mass mobilizations of appealing more to collective emotion than to individuality and hard work.

Throughout his life, Hoffer remained committed to retaining his own working-class identity. Even after he became a well-known public intellectual, Hoffer still worked on the docks. It was written that he "adhered to an ascetic* lifestyle, residing alone in a small, spartan* walk-up in a rooming-house atop one of Chinatown's steep hills, with no car, no telephone, and no television."[3] Although he wrote 12 books and many articles, Hoffer rejected the label of "intellectual." Instead, he insisted he was first and foremost a longshoreman. His extremely accessible writing style reflects the way he saw himself, and led to him being nicknamed the "Longshoreman Philosopher."

## NOTES

1   Eric Hoffer, *The Temper of Our Time* (New York: Hopewell Publications, 1976).

2   Tom Bethell, *Eric Hoffer: The Longshoreman Philosopher* (Stanford, CA: Hoover Institution Press, 2012), 27–47.

3   Tom Shachtman, *American Iconoclast: The Life and Times of Eric Hoffer* (New York: Hopewell Publications, 2011).

# MODULE 2
## ACADEMIC CONTEXT

### KEY POINTS

- In the 1950s, many scholars were trying to understand why people joined "mass movements."*

- When Hoffer wrote his text, some scholars saw the authoritarian* appeal of fascism* as some sort of moral failing in society; others saw it as a product of class struggle, a sociological change in society, or a psychological reaction in the mind.

- *The True Believer* combines sociological approaches (looking at society) and psychological analyses (investigating the mind) to understand why urban masses become both radicalized and involved in politics.

### The Work in its Context

In the 1930s and 1940s—before Eric Hoffer wrote *The True Believer: Thoughts on the Nature of Mass Movements*—Americans commonly spoke of "mass movements." But the phrase has largely fallen out of popular use. Modern writers might use any number of words to describe the phenomena Hoffer analyzes, including: "populist* movements," "uprisings," "terrorist groups," "radical organizations," "extremists," and "grassroots mobilizations."

But in the lead up to and aftermath of World War II,* many seemingly spontaneous political movements arose that appealed largely to the urban poor. This sparked widespread concern among people outside these movements. Political philosophers, sociologists, and psychologists at the time believed these "amorphous* masses" (or unstructured groups) operated according to different rules than other

**❝ I never had the urge to write until after I read Montaigne. ❞**
Eric Hoffer, in Calvin Thomas, *Eric Hoffer: An American Odyssey*

groups, like civic organizations or social classes. The latter could be counted on more or less to pursue their own rational goals but "the masses" were governed by fickle sentiments that skillful leaders could easily manipulate. Individuals who became part of these crowds lost their individual identity, as something like a mob mentality took over.

The entry of the masses into the political arena in the mid-twentieth century presented a substantial challenge to the political elite. They were used to a liberal-democratic* tradition based on a rather dispassionate, rational debate. But as the Spanish liberal* philosopher José Ortega y Gasset* warned his readers, these new mass political movements were characterized by the first appearance of "a type of man who does not want to give reasons or to be right, but simply shows himself resolved to impose his opinions. That is the new thing: the right not to be reasonable, the 'reason of unreason.'"[1] It seemed politics now lay in the hands of a crowd that could be easily manipulated. People caught up in a mass movement responded more to psychological influence or emotional appeals—the mob mentality—than to rational requests or reasoned arguments. Scholars would have to develop new ways to explain this kind of politics.

**Overview of the Field**
Where did fascism—an authoritarian, dictatorial form of right-wing government—come from? In the years before and after World War II, many political theorists, psychologists, and sociologists focused on that question, with debates that generally took one of four approaches.[2] First, American sociologist Peter Drucker* and others analyzed fascism as a moral failure on the part of the societies in which it took

root. The European political model had failed to pursue its founding principles of freedom and equality, and this allowed Nazism* and fascism to establish themselves in Germany and Italy, respectively.[3] A second group of authors, influenced by politically left-wing Marxist* analyses, saw fascism as the product of class struggle. Scholars like R. Palme Dutt* believed that Italy and Germany had fallen to fascism because capitalism* had come to dominate other types of economic production, leading to many ordinary people becoming disgruntled and angry.[4]

Two other schools of thought had more influence on Hoffer. A group of scholars, influenced heavily by Freudian* psychoanalysis,* (theories of the mind associated with the famous Austrian Sigmund Freud)* looked for the origins of fascism in the psychological defects of the people who were drawn to it. These scholars felt that something in the recent past must have caused large numbers of people to become susceptible to manipulation. Finally, a diverse group of academics focused on the entry of "amorphous masses," lacking any clear organizing principle or focus, into politics. A strong leader could easily manipulate people who had never before wielded any political power. *The True Believer* is in part an attempt to bring together these latter two schools of thought.

## Academic Influences

As a self-educated man, Hoffer did not have ties to any one school of academic thought, and neither does his text. Like his wider body of writing, *The True Believer* has diverse influences. However, these influences can only be seen indirectly, or by reading Hoffer's private notebooks. Not being a professional academic, he did not provide comprehensive footnotes or a literary review section.

Hoffer was a long-time admirer of the sixteenth-century French Renaissance* philosopher and essayist Michel de Montaigne,* and his informal and anecdotal writing style has a lot in common with

Montaigne's. Both writers make their general arguments by looking at real life. Montaigne, often described as a forefather of those who study modern psychology, wrote about the nature of belief, fear, happiness, and experience. Like Hoffer, the Frenchman did not try to develop a systematic approach to the individual. Instead, he formed his ideas about people based on what he saw, and what he thought about what he saw.

Although Hoffer rejected the ideas of Sigmund Freud, *The True Believer* also displays the influence of popular psychoanalytic ideas from the 1940s and 1950s. He took extensive notes on German psychologist Erich Fromm's* 1941 work, *Escape From Freedom*, another text that focused on the complex relationship between freedom, helplessness, and authoritarian politics. Like Hoffer, Fromm argued that people who submit themselves to an authority figure do so out of a sense of powerlessness and isolation. In return, they receive a sense of security and of belonging but the individual pays a high price: "He pays for the new security by giving up the integrity of his self."[5] In other words, he gives up his individual identity.

## NOTES

1   José Ortega y Gasset, *Revolt of the Masses* (New York: W. W. Norton and Co., 1993), 73.

2   A. James Gregor, *Interpretations of Fascism* (Morristown, NJ: General Learning Press, 1974), 20.

3   Peter Drucker, *The End of Economic Man: The Origins of Totalitarianism* (New York: Harper & Row, 1969).

4   Rajani Palme Dutt, *Fascism: An Analysis* (Allahabad: India Publishers, 1943).

5   Eric Fromm, *Escape From Freedom* (New York: Holt Paperbacks, 2008), 236.

# MODULE 3
## THE PROBLEM

### KEY POINTS

- Hoffer's *The True Believer* attempts to describe the common factors that give rise to all mass movements,* whether religious, political, or ideological in nature.

- Other scholars saw the political doctrine of fascism* as stemming from psychological traumas, the increasing isolation of individuals from one another, or a breakdown of common sense.

- Hoffer extended his analysis of fascism to cover all mass movements, whether they had positive or negative effects on the world.

### Core Question

Eric Hoffer titled the manuscript he submitted to publisher Harper's Press, *Thoughts on the Nature of Mass Movements.* They changed the title to *The True Believer*, demoting Hoffer's words to the subtitle. But Hoffer's original title perhaps reflects the central concerns of the text better than its published name. He wrote the book to try to explain the causes and development of what he calls "mass movements"—or what analysts today call "radical" or "extremist" movements.

Unlike other authors of the time, Hoffer was not merely interested in fascist or totalitarian* movements. He also looked at far less violent movements, like Mohandas Karmachand "Mahatma" Gandhi's* openly nonviolent movement to gain Indian independence* from British colonialism. Whether they are considered good or bad, Hoffer argues that we should analyze all mass movements according to the same criteria. As he explained, his book "does not maintain that all

> ❝ Though there are obvious differences between the fanatical Christian, the fanatical Mohammedan, the fanatical nationalist, the fanatical Communist and the fanatical Nazi, it is yet true that the fanaticism which animates them may be viewed and treated as one and the same. ❞
>
> Eric Hoffer, *The True Believer*

movements are identical, but that they share certain characteristics which give them a family likeness."[1]

The most significant thing all mass movements have in common, Hoffer argues, is the psychological profile of those who join them. Hoffer devotes most of *The True Believer* to detailing the reasons extremist groups appeal to the downtrodden. He also sees many of the same traits in their leaders' personalities, as well as in the stages of development that all mass movements pass through.

## The Participants

Hoffer was far from the first author to analyze the origins of fascism. Scholars generally agreed that fascism rose as less-educated city-dwellers suddenly became active in European politics for the first time. But what caused these urbanites to become attracted to fascism? Scholars disagreed on this.

One of the first people to identify the problem of the "amorphous* crowds" (meaning large groups lacking any clear, organizing principle, structure, or focus) was French psychologist and sociologist Gustave Le Bon.* As far back as 1895, Le Bon identified a new group of people motivated not by the rational interests of their social positions, but instead by emotional forces that drove them towards rage, unity, and extremism.[2] Le Bon became a major influence on twentieth-century studies of fascism. In 1942, the American sociologist Talcott

Parsons* blamed increasing "anomie"*—that is, isolation from social rules of behavior—for the growing number of people "imbued with a highly emotional, indeed often fanatical, zeal for a cause."[3] By contrast, psychologists like Peter Nathan* and Wilhelm Reich* understood fascism as developing from psychological traumas experienced by individuals.[4] In Germany and Italy, they argued, children had generally been brought up with a lower sense of self-esteem.* Throughout their adult lives this generated feelings of fear and inferiority, as well as a strong lust for power.

### The Contemporary Debate

Hoffer was one of the first authors to put forward a theory that could explain why individuals joined *any* mass movement—whether political, religious, or ideological.

When *The True Believer* was published in 1951, conventional wisdom said that Nazism* and Stalinism* were ideologically opposed. This seemed logical. After all, the two had been on opposite sides during World War II.* Hoffer, however, connected Nazism and Stalinism, though he was not the first thinker to do so. The same year that The True Believer appeared, political theorist Hannah Arendt* published her book, *The Origins of Totalitarianism*. Because she had been born a Jew in Germany, this issue was particularly important to Arendt. Like Hoffer, she argued that fascism arose in part because of the loss of a sense of community among masses of common people. With this breakdown in social relations also came a breakdown in "common sense,"[5] leaving people vulnerable to the "tribal nationalism"[6] that motivated both Nazism and Stalinism. Unlike Hoffer, Arendt believed that Nazism and Stalinism shared a common totalitarian thread that could not be generalized to other political movements. What Hoffer did was provide a framework capable of analyzing not only political movements like Nazism or Stalinism, but also fanatical religious groups, independence movements, and other social organizations. Hoffer had a friendly enough relationship with Arendt when the two both taught at the University of California, Berkeley but in his private notebooks he criticized her for being "consistently wrong in her explanations and predictions."[7]

## NOTES

1   Eric Hoffer, *The True Believer: Thoughts on the Nature of Mass Movements* (New York: Harper & Row, 1951), ix.

2   Gustave Le Bon, *The Crowd: A Study of the Popular Mind* (New York: Viking, 1960).

3   Talcott Parsons, *Essays in Sociological Theory* (New York: Free Press, 1949), 125.

4   Peter Nathan, *The Psychology of Fascism* (New York: Faber, 1943); Wilhelm Reich *The Mass Psychology of Fascism* (New York: Orgone Institute Press, 1946).

5   Hannah Arendt, *The Origins of Totalitarianism* (New York: Harcourt, 1973), 475.

6   Arendt, *The Origins of Totalitarianism,* 261.

7   Tom Bethell, *Eric Hoffer: The Longshoreman Philosopher* (Stanford, CA: oover Institution Press, 2012), 181.

# MODULE 4
# THE AUTHOR'S CONTRIBUTION

## KEY POINTS

- In *The True Believer,* Eric Hoffer tries to describe the characteristics that all mass movements* have in common.

- Hoffer expanded previous approaches to explaining fascism* to cover not only political mobilizations, but also religious groups, nationalist* movements, and ideological causes.

- Hoffer focused on the psychology of people attracted to radical political groups.

### Author's Aims

In *The True Believer: Thoughts on the Nature of Mass Movements*, Eric Hoffer writes, "This book deals with some peculiarities common to all mass movements, be they religious movements, social revolutions or nationalist movements. It does not maintain that they are identical, but that they share certain essential characteristics which give them a family likeness."[1] He was aiming to detail the elements all mass movements have in common.

Hoffer primarily focuses on the psychological factors that cause a person to join a mass movement that will rub out his or her individuality. For Hoffer, the best understanding of a mass movement does not come from examining its ideas, its leaders, or its organization. Instead, Hoffer argues that all mass movements attract the same frustrated personality type. He spends the majority of the book detailing the psychological profile of the type of people who sustain all kinds of radical groups.

Hoffer's secondary focus is on the dynamics that sustain these

> 66 Though they seem at opposite poles, fanatics of all kinds are actually crowded together at one end. It is the fanatic and the moderate who are poles apart and never meet. 99

Eric Hoffer, *The True Believer*

groups. Once people join a mass movement, what sorts of psychological factors then cause them to devote themselves so wholeheartedly to the cause—and even be willing to sacrifice their own lives in a belief that it will help the group reach its goals? Hoffer views the leaders as relatively unimportant to the success or otherwise of mass movements. Nevertheless, he devotes some time to profiling the people who begin those movements, those who lead them through their most active and dynamic phases, and those who bring the movement's emotional excesses under control.

## Approach

*The True Believer* is a broad and wide-ranging work. Hoffer takes a sweeping, impressionistic* approach, drawing lessons from his observations of contemporary political movements as well as from historical events. He does not base his work on a systematic examination of radicals or on statistical data. Instead, Hoffer sketches the outlines of his topic so that future researchers and politicians may use his ideas. Reflecting this approach, *The True Believer* does not look to derive general rules by exploring any one mass movement in particular. Instead, Hoffer sprinkles his writings with brief and diverse examples that illustrate his arguments. This observational style may be the text's greatest strength.

In Hoffer's day, formal psychological studies claimed that fascism developed either out of a certain type of parenting that drove children to become supporters of fascism later in life, or out of certain fundamental cultural traits. These views have now fallen out of fashion. By contrast, Hoffer's sketch of the psychological needs radical movements fulfill now seems way ahead of its time. Hoffer looked at how fascism spoke to frustrated individuals, provided their lives with purpose, and encouraged their loyalty to the group, even to the point where they became willing to sacrifice their lives for it. This comprehensive examination builds a compelling analysis that has endured well beyond the specific mass movements that inspired Hoffer to write this text in the first place.

## Contribution in Context

Hoffer was not the first author to analyze the rise of fascist politics. But he took a very innovative approach to mass movements. We can read Hoffer as synthesizing the four main understandings of fascism that existed at the time. Like the Marxists,* Hoffer believed that certain economic factors helped to increase the number of people susceptible to this kind of mass politics. The poor were especially likely to feel frustrated with their station in life. From the psychologists, Hoffer borrowed the idea that fascist movements addressed a sense of inadequacy and low self-esteem* characteristic of many people in modern city life. From political sociologists Hoffer drew the idea that the art of government changed substantially when irrational and easily swayed mobs entered politics. Finally, Hoffer is clear in his condemnation of fascism, seeing it as a great moral crisis and as a failure of modern politics.

But Hoffer's most innovative approach to the problem remains his expansion of our understanding of the concept of the "mass movement." Like his contemporaries, his most immediate concerns centered on Nazi* Germany, Mussolini's* Italy, and Stalinist* Russia but Hoffer extended his analysis well beyond the traditional focus on these specific groups. For Hoffer, a mass movement can be anything from a religious group to a political revolution or a national liberation movement.

Although he draws most of the examples in The True Believer from Nazi Germany and Soviet Russia,* Hoffer also discusses many other examples of mass movements, including the eighteenth-century French Revolution,* Zionism* (the political movement looking to establish a homeland for the Jewish people), Gandhi's* independence movement against British colonialism* in India, the religions of Roman Catholicism and early Islam,* Dixiecrats,* (a short-lived American political party dedicating to maintaining states' rights to segregation), and Zulus,* who also fought against British colonialism.

## NOTES

1   Eric Hoffer, *The True Believer: Thoughts on the Nature of Mass Movements* (New York: Harper & Row, 1951), xi.

# SECTION 2
## IDEAS

# MODULE 5
# MAIN IDEAS

## KEY POINTS

- *The True Believer* focuses on the nature of mass movements\* and the psychological profile of those who join them.
- Hoffer argues that these mass movements fulfill a basic psychological need for frustrated and hopeless individuals.
- *The True Believer* is a highly accessible work, aimed at readers with any level of education.

### Key Themes

In *The True Believer: Thoughts on the Nature of Mass Movements,* Eric Hoffer argues that we cannot explain mass movements, or radical groups, by the ideas they promote. In his view, people join extremist groups not because of their particular ideology, but because they need to fulfill a basic psychological need. They will grasp at any means necessary to escape their own persistent sense of despair: "Their innermost craving is for a new life—a rebirth—or, failing this, a chance to acquire new elements of pride, confidence, hope, a sense of purpose and worth by an identification with a holy cause."[1]

Having lost all hope in their own abilities, their self-worth, and their future prospects, these downtrodden individuals seek something that can give their lives meaning again: "When our individual prospects do not seem worth living for, we are in desperate need of something apart from ourselves to live for."[2] Mass movements provide something external towards which these despairing people can redirect their will to live.

Mass movements do not offer any kind of true psychological

**❝** The fanatic is perpetually incomplete and insecure. He cannot generate self-assurance out of his individual resources—out of his rejected self—but finds it only by clinging passionately to whatever support he happens to embrace. **❞**

Eric Hoffer, The True Believer

healing for these people, though. Instead, the movements magnify their problems. Radical organizations channel the individual's sense of frustration into a broader dissatisfaction with, and even hatred of, the current state of affairs: "Not only does a mass movement depict the present as mean and miserable—it deliberately makes it so."[3] Its members must therefore destroy the present to create a radically different society. Increasing the loss of self-esteem* that causes individuals to join extremist groups, mass movements promote a sense of unity and desire for self-sacrifice among their devotees: "Faith in a holy cause is to a considerable extent a substitute for the lost faith in ourselves."[4] When the life of any one individual is seen to be less valuable than the mission of the group, then any group member should be willing to fight and, if necessary, die for the cause.

In locating the origin of mass movements in the psychological desperation of frustrated individuals, Hoffer maintains that extremist groups are fundamentally alike. They may say they have different beliefs and ideas, but they all fulfill the same basic psychological needs. Hoffer argues, "When people are ripe for a mass movement, they are usually ripe for any effective movement, and not solely for one with a particular doctrine or program."[5] Because all such movements are competing for the same pool of frustrated individuals, radical movements play a zero-sum game. That means each radical movement's gain or loss is balanced by the losses or gains of another radical movement. If somebody joins a radical religious cult,* for instance, that person ceases to be available for recruitment by a radical political organization.

## Exploring the Ideas

Hoffer argued that mass movements start with people who have stopped believing in themselves and have lost all hope for their own future. Desperate to create some sort of meaning in their own lives, these people gravitate to new and radical causes. With no hope for their own future, they are willing to abandon their own sense of individual identity and replace it with a desire for unity and self-sacrifice. Hoffer writes, "the true believer who is wholly assimilated into a compact collective body is no longer frustrated. He has found a new identity and a new life" to replace his old one.[6]

As part of this "collective body," a person acquires a faith in their ability "to attack the past in order to liberate the present … [and] give up enthusiastically any chance of ever tasting or inheriting the present."[7] Instead, the true believer totally dedicates himself to a radically different future unconnected to the older traditions. Unquestioning devotion to a radical doctrine gives the follower a sense of power and purpose.

Hoffer identifies a number of things that can cause frustrated people to become vulnerable to recruitment by mass movements. Economic factors like poverty, especially among people who were not previously poor, can cause the type of deep frustrations that mass movements thrive on. The same psychological profile of frustration can also result from individual moral failings. People who are overly ambitious, selfish, sinners, or people who are simply just bored, are easy targets for recruitment. Minorities, faced with what seems like an impossible task of fully integrating into the dominant culture, can become frustrated when they see opportunities to improve their lives closed off to them.

Mass movements have their origins in the psychology of

frustrated individuals. But Hoffer also shows how these groups magnify the negative qualities that radicalized these people in the first place. These movements channel people's frustration and hopelessness. They encourage them to become fully dedicated to the group—with a dedication that exceeds even their commitment to themselves. This is how people become willing to sacrifice their own lives for the group. Hoffer pays particular attention to the ways radical groups bring their followers together by encouraging hatred: "Passionate hatred can give meaning and purpose to empty life."[8] It is not only people's dedication to the causes put forward by the group, but also their shared fanatical rejection of existing ideas or people that causes radical groups to stick together.

### Language and Expression

*The True Believer* is a highly accessible work, as we might expect from a self-educated thinker with deep working-class roots. Hoffer despised what he called "the German disease of making things difficult,"[9] blaming the impenetrability of scholars like the late eighteenth-century philosopher Georg Wilhelm Friedrich Hegel* for the rise of Nazism.* Hoffer emphasized the need for simplicity, both in his ideas and in his writing style. He wanted his book to be understandable not only to the professors who would take up his ideas, but also to politicians and his fellow laborers.

Yet the same casual style that makes the book so easy to read can also make it difficult to analyze. Hoffer gave *The True Believer* a loose structure. It seems closer to a series of observations than a rigorously developed, book-length argument. While Hoffer uses an impressively diverse array of anecdotes to provide evidence for his points, he does not examine these examples in much detail. At times this leads to some vagueness about what a true mass movement actually is. Still, this informal style has helped make the book a lasting success both inside and outside academia. Hoffer's observational style and quotable prose has drawn subsequent generations to his book each time a new radical organization emerges.

## NOTES

1   Eric Hoffer, *The True Believer: Thoughts on the Nature of Mass Movements* (New York: Harper & Row, 1951), 12.

2   Hoffer, *The True Believer*, 15.

3   Hoffer, *The True Believer*, 68.

4   Hoffer, *The True Believer*, 14.

5   Hoffer, *The True Believer*, 16.

6   Hoffer, *The True Believer*, 123–4.

7   Hoffer, *The True Believer*, 68.

8   Hoffer, *The True Believer*, 96

9   Tom Bethell, *Eric Hoffer: The Longshoreman Philosopher* (Stanford, CA: Hoover Institution Press, 2012), 224.

# MODULE 6
# SECONDARY IDEAS

## KEY POINTS

- Hoffer argues that all mass movements* follow the same developmental path, with each phase of a mass movement characterized by having a different kind of leader.

- Hoffer believes that all mass movements stem from the same psychological needs of disenchanted people. But the specific shape a mass movement takes depends on its leaders.

- Despite his skepticism about the nature of mass movements, Hoffer did not believe all of them were evil. He saw that on occasion a mass movement can be a necessary force for renewal.

### Other Ideas

In *The True Believer: Thoughts on the Nature of Mass Movements,* Eric Hoffer argues that all mass movements follow a similar pathway. Hoffer divides the rise and fall of extremist groups into three distinct phases.

During the first phase, mass movements gather strength as mounting frustration leads more people to join extremist groups. Once a movement builds up enough followers, it enters what Hoffer calls its "active phase." This is when the movement is at its most fanatical and most dangerous, when the characteristics of unity and self-sacrifice that define mass movements burn most intensely. Eventually, the movement becomes moderated. Perhaps the authorities successfully repress it, in which case the movement's followers will likely remain frustrated, with trouble liable to flare up again. Or perhaps the movement achieves its goals. In that case, we can count on a new group of frustrated people to

> 66 The personality of the leader is probably a crucial factor in determining the nature and duration of a mass movement. Such rare leaders as Lincoln and Gandhi not only try to curb the evil inherent in a mass movement but are willing to put an end to the movement when its objective is more or less realized. 99
>
> Eric Hoffer, *The True Believer*

come together in yet another movement. The issues highlighted by mass movements may change but Hoffer recognizes that the phenomenon of mass movements will never disappear.

Hoffer believes that mass movements stem from the frustrations of individuals. while also devoting a considerable space in the book to analyzing the role of populist* leaders. Although these leaders do not determine whether a mass movement will form, they are crucial in shaping the particular form of the mass movement and steering it through its three stages of development. Hoffer divides these leaders into three categories: men of words during the initial phase of the movement; fanatics in the active phase; and practical men of action as the movement becomes more tamed. These leaders do not have to be three separate individuals, rather these are the three roles that leaders must adopt as movements develop and change over time. Most leaders—such as Vladimir Lenin,* who led the Russian Revolution of 1917*—are incapable of making the transition from one role to another. Usually, their successors kill them off. But that violent transition may actually be good for the cause. As Hoffer notes, "When the same person or persons (or the same type of person) leads a movement from its inception to maturity, it usually ends in disaster."[1] On very rare occasions, great leaders like US president Abraham Lincoln* will have the self-confidence to end the active phase of a mass movement themselves, and then go on to construct a new order.

## Exploring the Ideas

As they fulfill their roles in the mass movement, the three types of leaders display markedly different characteristics.

"Men of words" are intellectuals who see themselves as representatives of the downtrodden and oppressed. By criticizing the authorities, they make the discontented question their beliefs and their loyalty to existing institutions. Often, these men of words also provide the slogans of revolution. Although they lay the groundwork for mass movements, Hoffer sees men of words as tragic figures. As intellectuals, they are naturally individualistic in their thinking. Unlike their followers, they cannot let their own will be absorbed into that of the group, so they often wind up the victims of the very movements they themselves sparked.

"Fanatics" are still the key figures in any mass movement. "When the moment is ripe, only the fanatic can hatch a genuine mass movement. Without him, the disaffection engendered by militant men of words remains undirected."[2] These leaders kick off the "active phase" of the mass movement, when its destructive tendencies are at their fullest. Although fanatics lack the creativity of the men of words, they know how to read a crowd, and control and direct their desires: "He alone knows the innermost craving of the masses in action: the craving for communion, for the mustering of the host, for the dissolution of cursed individuality in the majesty and grandeur of the mighty whole."[3] The fanatic may also provoke people in ways he cannot control. Since the mass movement itself breeds hatred and searches out more and more enemies in its unceasing quest for extremism, the risk remains that the movement will become even more violent, and so need a leader with yet more bloodlust.

The practical "man of action" saves the movement from its own destructive tendencies. These leaders put an end to the "active phase" of the mass movement. They consolidate it into new institutions, such as state bureaucracies or Church hierarchies. Emphasizing a sense of duty, the man of action cultivates the people's sense of loyalty to the new establishment. Driven by purpose, the man of action is more of a pragmatist, willing to borrow from the enemy to achieve stability and durability: "He even goes back to the old order which preceded the movement and appropriates from it many techniques of stability, thus unintentionally establishing continuity with the past."[4]

While the man of action brings an end to a particular radical organization, this does not necessarily mean that the root causes of why the mass movement grew in the first place have been addressed. Once established, "the mass movement ceases to be a refuge from the agonies and burdens of an individual existence."[5] As long as society produces frustrated individuals, a new mass movement is bound to emerge.

### Overlooked

The ideas of *The True Believer* have recently returned to mainstream popularity to help explain radical Islamic terrorism. Hoffer does not view all mass movements as bad. On the contrary, he argues that they are at times necessary to revitalize a stagnant political community: "A genuine popular upheaval is often an invigorating, renovating and integrating process."[6] The frustration of the masses stems in part from the failures of their leaders and institutions. Sometimes a mass movement can fix these problems in the authority that already exists.

In the final, somewhat underdeveloped, section of his book, Hoffer tries to distinguish between good and bad mass movements. Although scholars rarely mention this section today, it does offer some ways to distinguish between positive and negative mass movements.

The most important distinction relates to the nature of the movement's goals. While good mass movements pursue concrete and realistic goals, bad mass movements phrase their aims vaguely.[7] Hoffer argues that positive mass movements are often characterized by the overthrow of a long-entrenched authority. All mass movements feature a tendency toward imitation and tend to promote self-denial.

Many uprisings, such as "the Reformation,* of the sixteenth century, the Puritan* attempts in sixteenth century England to rid the Church of England from Catholic influence, and also the American* and French revolutions* at the end of the eighteenth century, come to an end, after a relatively short active phase. The new social order that results tends to offer increased individual liberty."[8] In contrast, truly negative mass movements have vague goals. Without ever truly being able to achieve their fuzzy ideals, they drift toward authoritarianism.* They end up being in a permanent active phase without an endpoint. However, an exceptional leader such as Abraham Lincoln or Mohandas Karmachand "Mahatma" Gandhi* may be capable of curbing the destructive tendencies of mass movements and harnessing them towards positive goals. By the same token, a ruthless leader—a Hitler* or a Stalin* in the modern era, or an Oliver Cromwell,* the tyrannical Lord Protector of the Commonwealth after the English Civil War— may amplify the barbarity that is characteristic of mass movements.

## NOTES

1   *Eric Hoffer, The True Believer: Thoughts on the Nature of Mass Movements (New York: Harper & Row, 1951), 146.*

2   *Hoffer, The True Believer, 142.*

3   *Hoffer, The True Believer, 143.*

4   *Hoffer, The True Believer, 149.*

5   *Hoffer, The True Believer, 150.*

6   *Hoffer, The True Believer, 164.*

7   *Hoffer, The True Believer, 155–6.*

8   *Hoffer, The True Believer, 159–60.*

# MODULE 7
# ACHIEVEMENT

## KEY POINTS

- Eric Hoffer successfully changed the ways politicians and academics talked about mass movements.*

- Hoffer's focus on the psychology of those who join mass movements allowed policy-makers to focus on new areas.

- But Hoffer's vagueness makes it difficult to assess what qualifies as a mass movement and what does not.

### Assessing the Argument

Eric Hoffer's *The True Believer: Thoughts on the Nature of Mass Movements* does not set out to be an exhaustive study of extremist organizations. Hoffer's own description of the work reads, "This is not an authoritative textbook. It is a book of thoughts, and it does not shy away from half-truths so long as they seem to hint at a new approach and help to formulate new questions."[1]

Judged on these terms, Hoffer's book undoubtedly succeeds. He does not intend for the text to be read as a formal model or rule book that can be used to decide if any group is a mass movement or not. The book successfully shifts the discussion from the ideas that mass movements put forward to the conditions that produce their followers. At no point in the text does Hoffer concern himself with the *ideas* of Nazism* or Stalinism,* even though he clearly expresses his disdain for both movements. Instead, he asks the reader to consider what sorts of psychological states must exist in people for them to become open to such repulsive ideas. By shedding light on the question of how extremist groups fulfill certain psychological needs in individuals, Hoffer not only inspired ongoing research into fascism,* but also the

❝ If you want concise insight into what drives the mind of the fanatic and the dynamics of a mass movement at their most primal level, may I suggest an evening with Eric Hoffer. ❞

John McDonough, *Wall Street Journal*

creation of new counterterrorism strategies and deradicalization programs.

## Achievement in Context

*The True Believer* is very much the product of an American mind and of someone writing both during and after World War II.* At that time, both politicians and academics struggled to work out how the United States should relate to the Soviet Union,* which had been a US ally during World War II. In 1943, President Franklin Delano Roosevelt* famously declared his belief that Stalin "won't try to annex anything and will work with me for a world of democracy* and peace."[2] Hoffer was far more suspicious of the Soviet Union. His skepticism dated back to the 1939–41 nonaggression pact that was signed between Stalin and Hitler, and which of course was almost immediately broken.

Published in 1951, *The True Believer* quickly had a significant impact on public debate in the United States, and by 1967 had sold over half a million copies. It was reportedly one of President Dwight D. Eisenhower's* favorite books, and he urged his cabinet to read it and often gave copies to visitors. In a letter to a supporter, Eisenhower praised the book for demonstrating "that dictatorial systems make one contribution to their people which leads them to tend to support such systems—freedom from the necessity of informing themselves and making up their own minds."[3] Hoffer's arguments that mass movements appealed to the worst aspects of humanity, to our perceived inferiorities and fears, had entered into the mainstream and they would influence the thoughts of policy-makers for generations to come.

## Limitations

*The True Believer's* greatest strengths may also be its most significant limitations. Hoffer writes in a relatively ill-defined style. For instance, he keeps his definition of a mass movement intentionally imprecise, which makes his arguments difficult to argue against. Rather than produce a detailed analysis of any one radical group, Hoffer chooses to emphasize the qualities that unify all mass movements. When the book was first published, critics saw this as a major oversight. One reviewer commented, "The more I think about the book, the more strongly I feel that what it needs most is a more precise definition of mass movements, to distinguish them clearly from other kinds of group undertakings which often bring about important changes but are not so strongly characterized by the phenomenon of the 'true believer.'"[4] Because Hoffer never actually defined his key term, it is still impossible to tell if populist* movements that sprang up later—like the 1960s subculture of hippies,* the Civil Rights Movement* in the United States of the 1950s and 1960s,* or the anti-Vietnam War protests* of the 1960s and 1970s—qualify as mass movements or not.

*The True Believer* gives us a way to analyze the psychological and social conditions that generate radical political thought. Quite deliberately, it does not offer a way to analyze the ideas that inspire such action. Hoffer provides no framework to help us work out when radical political action may be justified or necessary. Instead he sees all mass movements as stemming from the same roots: psychological frustration and loss of individuality by those who are followers. By doing this, Hoffer argues that people do not, in fact, choose their own destiny and their own political movements. This means his analysis ignores the bravery or wisdom of the individuals who fought in "positive" mass movements for ideas, rights, and policies that were once considered outside the political mainstream.

Not surprisingly, people who are involved in political or religious organizations have often taken offense at being classified as being part of a mass movement. The label suggests they did not rationally choose to follow ideas. Instead, Hoffer implies that their devotion is the random display of a fundamental mental inadequacy.

Hoffer also frequently displays prejudice. He sees different races and nationalities as being characterized by distinct psychological dispositions,* or tendencies. Unlike people who believe in scientific racism,* Hoffer rejects the idea that these differences are because of inborn biological differences between the races. Instead, he argues that different national characteristics stem from each particular group's long and unique history. For instance, in *The True Believer* Hoffer writes, "The fact is that the Japanese, Russians and Germans, who allow the interminable continuation of an active mass movement with a show of opposition, were inured to submissiveness or iron discipline for generations before the rise of their mass movements."[5] Regardless of why he does so, Hoffer's tendency to assign psychological traits to entire groups of people can, at times, now be perceived as shades of racism, especially in some of his subsequent works.

## NOTES

1 Eric Hoffer, *The True Believer: Thoughts on the Nature of Mass Movements* (New York: Harper & Row, 1951), 59.

2 Fred Charles Iklé, *How Nations Negotiate* (New York: Harper & Row, 1964), 89.

3 Max Blumenthal, "Ike's Other Warning," *New York Times*, September 2, 2009, accessed October 22, 2015, http://www.nytimes.com/2009/09/03/opinion/03blumenthal.html.

4 Tom Bethell, *Eric Hoffer: The Longshoreman Philosopher* (Stanford, CA: Hoover Institution Press, 2012), 117.

5 Hoffer, *The True Believer*, 158.

# MODULE 8
# PLACE IN THE AUTHOR'S WORK

## KEY POINTS

- After *The True Believer* was published, Hoffer continued to focus on the connections between psychology and politics.

- *The True Believer* remains Hoffer's best-known work and the most concise summary of his overall thinking.

- Later in his life, Hoffer sharpened his criticism of communists* and American intellectuals who were critical of America.

### Positioning

Published in 1951, *The True Believer: Thoughts on the Nature of Mass Movements* was Eric Hoffer's first book. The clarity of the ideas and the polished writing style—combined with Hoffer's incredible story as a self-educated working-class intellectual—quickly propelled the author to national fame. Initially unprepared for this sudden thrusting into the spotlight, Hoffer took time off from his job as a longshoreman to travel anonymously, visiting agricultural towns in California while still continuing to write. It was only when his third book, The Ordeal of Change,[1] was published 12 years later, in 1963, that Hoffer finally agreed to interviews on public radio stations and nationally syndicated television shows.

As mainstream American politics moved increasingly toward the left in the 1960s and 1970s, Hoffer would become a leading conservative* thinker. Emerging as a public intellectual, he would apply many of the insights he first developed in the pages of *The True Believer* to his fellow countrymen. He praised the American worker for hard work and independence. Yet at the same time, Hoffer worried that increasing automation and mechanization in the workplace might

> **❝ When America pulls through and revives its national pride there will be a flexing that will jar the new world from the North Pole to South. ❞**
>
> Eric Hoffer, quoted in Tom Bethell, *The Longshoreman Philosopher*

lead to "a dangerously volatile element in a totally new kind of American society"[2] by breeding precisely the sort of despair he warned against in his most famous work. Hoffer also criticized the liberal* countercultural movements of the day, including the Civil Rights Movement,* the Free Speech Movement,* and anti-Vietnam War protests.* He saw in these various political mobilizations many of the negative characteristics he first identified with mass movements* in 1951.

Yet Hoffer continued to see hope in at least some mass movements. Later in his life, he became a vocal supporter of Zionism,* the national political movement that sought to establish a homeland for the Jewish people, which he had identified as a mass movement in *The True Believer.* In his subsequent essays, as in the book that launched his career, Hoffer struggled to balance his great skepticism of populist* groups with their unparalleled ability to drive certain important historical changes.

### Integration

Hoffer remained interested in the psychological tendencies that gave rise to political movements. *The Ordeal of Change,* published in 1963, became his second most famous work, written against the backdrop of the Korean War* of 1950–3 where North Korea (backed by the Soviet Union)* fought South Korea (backed by the United States) in a battle of communism against democracy.* This collection of essays sets out to analyze the political problems that characterized Asia. Once again, Hoffer rejected his contemporaries' commonly accepted views.

At the time, political analysts traced the struggle between communist and capitalist* forces in Asia to a combination of the violence of colonialism,* the agitation of communist agents, or the corruption of local officials. Hoffer, however, argued that Asian peoples had a "craving for pride."[3] Mirroring his arguments from sections of *The True Believer*, Hoffer argues in *The Ordeal of Change* that the erosion of traditional family structures in Asia created feelings of self-loathing. This low self-esteem,* in turn, fostered an intense desire for change, to the point where Asians became willing to sacrifice their own lives to create a radically different sort of world: "Living barren, useless lives, they are without self-confidence and self-respect, and their craving is for the illusion of weight and importance, and for the explosive substitutes of pride and faith."[4]

Hoffer touched on the Soviet Union in *The True Believer*, but in later works he would become more critical of communism. In his essay "The Readiness to Work," Hoffer argues that the main challenge for communism was "how to make people work—how to induce them to plow, sow, harvest, build, manufacture."[5] By contrast, in the West, individual freedom gave the masses a motivation to work hard and make the most of their individuality. Once again, the key difference between the two economic systems, for Hoffer, lies in their psychological appeal to workers. As his writing matured, Hoffer increasingly emphasized the importance of individual liberty as a key motivation for the working masses.

American public intellectuals grew increasingly critical of their country in the 1960s and 1970s, but Hoffer moved in the opposite direction. He accused many public scholars of selfishness and of simply wanting to be famous. By contrast, Hoffer grew increasingly convinced of American exceptionalism* throughout his career. In his final press interview in 1983, Hoffer declared, "America is a nation that has run on morals, almost independent of its leaders or Congress. For a long time America didn't need a government. People from all over the world came here, worked hard and made America work."[6] To the very end, the character of the people, rather than of their leaders, mattered most to Hoffer.

## Significance

The success of *The True Believer* propelled Hoffer to national acclaim and he became a much sought-after public intellectual. This owed as much to his incredible life as to the power of his ideas. He was interviewed on television—both on major broadcast networks and on public television, which catered to a smaller, more intellectual audience. *The New Yorker* magazine ran an extensive profile of him. After Robert F. Kennedy's* assassination in 1968, President Lyndon B. Johnson* appointed Hoffer to the National Commission on the Causes and Prevention of Violence.* He proved to be a controversial figure because of his vocal criticisms of Civil Rights leaders. Hoffer accused them of encouraging rage in the African American community and of failing to build communal institutions. In 1983, President Ronald Reagan* awarded Hoffer the Presidential Medal of Freedom.*

In the second half of the twentieth century, *The True Believer* slowly fell out of fashion. As the Cold War* developed, scholars and politicians focused less on dealing with radical fringe groups and instead devoted their attention to managing the delicate balance between the superpowers of the United States and the Soviet Union. However, following radical Islamic terrorist group al-Qaeda's* attacks on the United States on September 11, 2001,* the book was rushed back into print. Suddenly, the exact same questions that had motivated Hoffer to write *The True Believer* once again occupied the public's imagination. Hoffer's writings on radical mass movements provided an important starting point for people to examine why some are prepared to volunteer for death in the service of an extremist ideology.

## NOTES

1   Eric Hoffer, *The Ordeal of Change* (New York: Buccaneer Books, 1976).

2   Tom Bethell, *Eric Hoffer: The Longshoreman Philosopher* (Stanford, CA: Hoover Institution Press), 134.

3   Hoffer, *Ordeal of Change*, 8.

4   Hoffer, *Ordeal of Change*, 11.

5   Hoffer, *Ordeal of Change*, 30.

6   Gene Grissman, "The Weariness of a True Believer: Eric Hoffer's Parting Words," *San Francisco Chronicle*, July 10, 1983.

# SECTION 3
# IMPACT

# MODULE 9
# THE FIRST RESPONSES

## KEY POINTS

- Scholars criticized *The True Believer* for not offering a more precise definition of mass movements* and for casually dismissing the beliefs of political activists and religious devotees.

- Hoffer rejected calls for precision, preferring to let others adapt his ideas in their own thinking.

- Later in his life Hoffer became willing to reconsider whether certain groups he characterized as "mass movements" truly fit the category after all.

### Criticism

Both the popular press and academic scholars praised Eric Hoffer's *The True Believer: Thoughts on the Nature of Mass Movements* when it was published in 1951. Harvard University-based historian Arthur Schlesinger* called it "brilliant and original."[1] From Cambridge University, the famous philosopher Bertrand Russell* praised Hoffer's work as "sound intellectually and timely politically."[2] Reviews of the book commented on its accessible writing style. *The New York Herald Tribune* newspaper called Hoffer "a born essayist-philosopher."[3] His ability to approach such a controversial subject dispassionately, meanwhile, impressed the *New York Post* reviewer, who called the book "a model of detachment about the kind of person who has generally lent himself to anything but detachment."[4]

On the other hand, several people associated with groups Hoffer labels as "mass movements" immediately and passionately rejected the book. People with ties to the Socialist Party,* like Evan Thomas*—

> **❝** To think out a problem is not unlike drawing a caricature. You have to exaggerate the salient point and leave out that which is not typical. **❞**
>
> Eric Hoffer, in Tom Bethell, *The Longshoreman Philosopher*

an acquisition editor at Hoffer's own publisher, Harper's—attacked the book for saying that all political action could be traced to a psychological loss of self-worth. These people said Hoffer left no room for people to hold any real belief in the positive potential of a radical movement.[5] Similarly, the Roman Catholic monk Bernard Theall* attacked the book for comparing religious movements to fascism* and communism.*[6]

More subtle criticisms centered on Hoffer's definition of a mass movement—or to be more accurate, his lack of a definition. Political science professor A. James Gregor* criticized works like Hoffer's for being overly vague: "at best, they provide broad and imprecise conceptual categories that perhaps assist us in identifying some of the necessary conditions for the advent of fascism."[7] Even many of the book's supporters agreed with this criticism. Historian Richard Pipes,* who assigned *The True Believer* in his Harvard classes, said that the book applied the term "mass movement" too loosely. Pipes viewed mass movements as relatively rare happenings that usually involved only a minority of the population—if only because the majority remained too concerned with their daily lives to actively engage in political activity.[8] Even Hoffer's biographer, Tom Bethell,* notes that readers of *The True Believer* sometimes encounter "a sea of abstractions … and many will have scanned its pages, often in vain, looking for the tall masts and capital letters of a proper name."[9] Although Hoffer made compelling generalizations, readers often struggle to understand how and where they may apply his observations to the real world.

## Responses

Hoffer did not respond directly to his critics. *The True Believer* made him famous, but initially he shunned the limelight, giving few interviews and public talks in the years after the book's publication.

Still, we may read Hoffer's subsequent work in part as a response to critics of *The True Believer*. Hoffer eventually accepted Dr. Pipes's position that mass movements only arise infrequently. He also moved away from his initial belief that the leaders of mass movements are relatively unimportant to those movements' development. In a 1967 interview, Hoffer seemed to reverse the position he laid out in *The True Believer*, declaring that "mass movements are not started by the masses. Mass movements are started by intellectuals."[10] Nonetheless, Hoffer continued to believe that extremist groups existed first and foremost as a response to the psychological needs of people who had lost faith in themselves.

Hoffer remained a lifelong atheist. He didn't believe in God, but as he matured he adopted a more respectful tone toward the religion of Christianity. By the end of his life, he had stopped referring to Christianity as a mass movement, and even praised it for promoting individual responsibility among those who followed it. Over the years, Hoffer increasingly turned his attention away from religious groups to focus on political movements—from communism to the anticolonial* militants fighting for independence in the 1970s. His work became extremely important again more than six decades after it was first published due to the rise of terrorist organizations killing in the name of Islam.*

## Conflict and Consensus

Hoffer would eventually find common ground with many of his early critics. The initial debate about the text focused on how to identify a mass movement, with Nazism* and Stalinism* being used as examples. At first, Hoffer seemed uninterested in the question of where to draw the line between mass movements and practical organizations but over time he became willing to modify his assessments of the latter.

What scholars once considered a major defect in Hoffer's work, however, has now become commonplace in conversations about terrorism and radical political organizations. Few scholars today devote time to classifying groups as either "mass movements" or "practical organizations." Instead, they look to Hoffer to explain the appeal of certain types of organizations that simply lie outside the mainstream.

Religious and political leaders also criticized *The True Believer* when it was first published. Though their arguments did not garner much attention at that time, they directly predicted modern controversies about the text. Today, scholars who take up Hoffer's approach sometimes find themselves accused of ignoring the stated missions of the mass movement. Hoffer focuses on the emotions and feelings that cause an individual to yearn for radical political change. But he provides no way of discerning whether that change is positive or negative, or whether it is justified or not. Were he alive today, Hoffer would see a Black Lives Matter* activist looking to challenge police violence against African Americans, a Tea Party* supporter wanting to reduce the influence of the US government, and an al-Qaeda* terrorist looking to fight for his religious beliefs as all motivated by the same underlying psychological issues.

## NOTES

1   Tom Bethell, *Eric Hoffer: The Longshoreman Philosopher* (Stanford, CA: Hoover Institution Press), 120.

2   Bethell, *Longshoreman Philosopher*, 120.

3   Brinton Crane, "Review of Eric Hoffer's *The True Believer*," *New York Herald Tribune*, quoted in Bethell, *Longshoreman Philosopher*, 120.

4   Bethell, *Longshoreman Philosopher*, 121.

5   Bethell, *Longshoreman Philosopher*, 124.

6   Bernard Theall, "When Does a Believer Become a Fanatic?" *Books on Trial*,

April 1951.

7   A. James Gregor, *Fascism: The Contemporary Interpretations* (Morristown, NJ: General Learning Corporation, 1973), 11.

8   Bethell, *Longshoreman Philosopher*, 126.

9   Bethell, *Longshoreman Philosopher,* 125.

10  "The Passionate State of Mind," CBS, broadcast hosted by Eric Sevareid, September 17, 1967.

# MODULE 10
## THE EVOLVING DEBATE

### KEY POINTS

- Hoffer's ideas led scholars to start paying attention to the role of individual psychology and self-esteem* in causing people to join radical movements.

- Hoffer showed that psychology could be just as important as economic or political motives in explaining the rise of mass movements.* But more recent scholarship has gone beyond simply looking at self-esteem as the root cause of these phenomena.

- New terrorism studies expand Hoffer's analysis to Islamic fundamentalism* by focusing on some of his underexplored ideas.

### Uses and Problems

Eric Hoffer's *The True Believer: Thoughts on the Nature of Mass Movements* had an enormous influence. It helped scholars, politicians, and interested readers to understand fascism* and the mindset that fuels the creation of mass movements and terror organizations. Hoffer was among the first to recognize that insecurity and a lack of self-esteem could lead people to overcompensate and even seek to dominate others. Some scholars argued that individuals might join fascist organizations because of poverty or a feeling that the dominant society exploited them in some way. Hoffer found the real drive behind fanaticism in an individual's own personal self-esteem helping to explain why even wealthy and well-established people sometimes choose to back radical movements.

Despite its enormous initial impact on public debate, *The True*

> **❝** The practice of terror serves the true believer not only to cow and crush his opponents but also to invigorate and intensify his own faith. **❞**
>
> Eric Hoffer, *The True Believer*

*Believer* began to fade into obscurity during the 1970s. But after the terror attacks of September 11, 2001 (9/11)\* the publisher rushed the book back into print. Contemporary analysts saw in Hoffer's text an important way to explain why so many young men voluntarily chose to die in the name of militant Islam.\* By going back to this long-forgotten book, scholars of terrorism found a rich analysis linking these young men's sense of frustration and inadequacy to their decision to join terror organizations.

This renewed, post-9/11 interest in *The True Believer* also prompted scholars to delve into previously underexplored parts of Hoffer's text. The debate that sprang up after the book was first published largely centered on Hoffer's proposal to look at opposing ideological movements as essentially the same. Scholars of modern terrorism are more interested in his insights into how mass movements sustain themselves and keep going. Drawing on Hoffer's psychological explanations, these analysts focus on the ways in which terror organizations cultivate hatred of the "other" and use this tactic to recruit new members. Modern critics of Islamic terrorism use Hoffer's work as a way to explain religious fundamentalism and frequently refer to Hoffer's observation that "[p]assionate hatred can give meaning and purpose to an empty life."[1]

## Schools of Thought

*The True Believer* convinced academics to focus on the psychological profile of people joining extremist movements. Hoffer's emphasis on the importance of self-esteem to an individual's well-being proved to be a significant contribution to the field of social psychology,* or how a social context shapes an individual's thoughts, emotions, and behavior. Wanting to explore the sociological dimensions of the mind, social psychologists particularly embraced Hoffer's theory of self-esteem. This theory continues to shape this important school of humanist psychology,* the branch of psychology that believes all people are naturally good. For example, psychotherapist Nathaniel Branden* used Hoffer's ideas to explain the psychological shortcomings of violent people: "longshoreman-philosopher Eric Hoffer remarks somewhere that the problem is that this is precisely what people do: Persons who hate themselves hate others. The killers of the world, literally and figuratively, are not known to be in loving relationships to their inner selves."[2]

Hoffer's work has had the most significant impact on politicians and popular commentators. His defense of American individualism* and self-reliance, his attacks on the radical political movements of the 1960s, and his passionate opposition to communism* made him a hero of the conservative* movement. For conservatives, Hoffer's own life story and his investigation of antidemocratic societies represented the very best of America's individualist tradition. President Eisenhower* embraced the newly published book in 1951 as the US tried to find its footing in relation to the Soviet Union.* Today the emergence of terror groups such as Islamic extremists ISIS* in the Middle East poses the most urgent threat. Modern-day conservatives find Hoffer's unflinching analysis of fanatical movements helps them understand the situation better.

Analysts trying to explain the near-simultaneous US rise of the Tea Party* (which opposes overly dominating government) and Occupy Wall Street* (which protests against growing economic inequality) have turned to *The True Believer*. A 2012 piece in the *New York Daily News* echoed many of Hoffer's insights from 60 years earlier. The writer argued that these two movements "aren't really that different at all. Both, in fact, hew to the same conventions as all mass movements."[3] Even the popular press now treats many of these ideas as conventional wisdom, which shows how far Hoffer's work has penetrated mainstream thinking.

### In Current Scholarship

*The True Believer* has quickly become an established text in the growing field of terrorism studies. Contemporary scholars have explored Hoffer's psychological model for a number of reasons. Chiefly, they want to explain why cultivating hatred for "others" appears to be such a powerful weapon for terror organizations in their attempts to recruit new members. Analysts of modern-day global terror networks agree with Hoffer. They suggest that these organizations get significant mileage from redirecting people's internal feelings of frustration and channeling it into hatred of an external enemy.

Hoffer also provides a useful way for counterterrorism scholars to explain why we cannot reason with terrorists. People who join radical movements because of their own low self-esteem will likely seek to overcompensate for their perceived failures by unconditionally following whatever cause they adopt. As a result, some of the most recent scholarship insists that we cannot explain terrorism as merely a byproduct of Islamic fundamentalism.

According to the philosopher Tim Madigan,* terrorism "goes far beyond a debate over religious beliefs, to the very heart of human nature: what allows certain people to override any sense of community with their fellow human beings, and willfully cause death and destruction for the sake of a higher cause?"[4] People will continue to debate these questions for as long as violent and radical movements exist.

# NOTES

1   Eric Hoffer, *The True Believer: Thoughts on the Nature of Mass Movements* (New York: Harper & Row, 1951), 96.

2   Nathaniel Branden, *Six Pillars of Self Esteem* (New York: Random House, 1995), 48.

3   S. E. Cupp, "What Occupy Wall Street and the Tea Party have in common: Right or left, all mass movements are the same," *New York Daily News,* November 16, 2011, accessed October 22, 2015, http://www.nydailynews. com/opinion/occupy-wall-street-tea-party-common-left-mass-movements-article-1.977949#ixzz2LRkultyc.

4   Tim Madigan, "The True Believer Revisited," *Philosophy Now* 34, accessed October 22, 2015, https://philosophynow.org/issues/34/The_True_ Believer_Revisited.

# MODULE 11
# IMPACT AND INFLUENCE TODAY

## KEY POINTS

- *The True Believer* may be more influential among policy-makers and psychologists today than at any point since its publication.
- Hoffer's text challenges us to look for the root causes of radicalism and terrorism in people's sense of self.
- In contrast to Hoffer, other terrorism scholars have approached terrorism as a tactic that rational people use to reach an objective.

### Position

More than a half-century after its publication, the ideas in Eric Hoffer's *The True Believer: Thoughts on the Nature of Mass Movements* still spark lively debate. After the terror attacks on New York of September 11, 2001\* (also known as 9/11), analysts sought to understand how al-Qaeda\* leader Osama bin Laden's\* ideas and violent methods could have attracted so many supporters worldwide. To answer this question, modern scholars of terrorism drew on Hoffer's analysis of Adolf Hitler's\* leadership in Nazi\* Germany in the first half of the twentieth century. The powerful presence of a leader like Bin Laden, they argue, allows otherwise "isolated and individually aggrieved" people to unite in a common cause. It says much about the depth of Hoffer's thinking that contemporary scholars can draw insights from a text written in a very different era to explain very different movements. This surely makes a solid case for the fact that Hoffer's work is still relevant.

While it has certainly helped fuel recent breakthroughs in the field of terrorism studies, we must bear in mind that Hoffer wrote *The True*

> **66** It has often been said that power corrupts. But it is perhaps equally important to realize that weakness, too, corrupts. Power corrupts the few, while weakness corrupts the many. **99**

Eric Hoffer, *The Passionate State of Mind*

*Believer* during a very different time. The main issues facing the world in 1951 were centralized state fascism* (though fascist rule had ended in Germany and Italy by this time) and totalitarian* rule. Hoffer could not have imagined, much less analyzed, the kinds of decentralized global networks that comprise modern-day terror organizations. Yet despite this, his text still adds much to our contemporary efforts to understand fanatical behavior.

## Interaction

*The True Believer* continues to shed light on a range of contemporary social problems. These range from newer topics like the rise of Islamic fundamentalism* and militant networks to more established neo-Nazi* organizations and other hate groups.

Hoffer's text has found particular support in the interdisciplinary combination of social psychology* and terror studies. Scholars like Jerrold Post,*[1] an expert in political psychology, use Hoffer's work to show that people who commit terror acts are not insane. Rather, they are rational individuals who actually appear "disturbingly normal."[2] *The True Believer* has also quickly become a major text in the emerging field of terrorism studies. Joe Navarro,* an author and former FBI* agent, writes, "Hoffer's paradigm* of mass movements* from sixty years ago still remains valid today. Mass movements, including terrorist movements, uniformly attract these all too familiar kinds of individuals, the dynamic-charismatic leader, the totally compliant follower, and the opportunistic criminal."[3]

One main reason why Hoffer's work has lasted is the uniqueness of his psychological model. A man ahead of his time, Hoffer broke with American psychology's long-standing reliance on Freudian* explanations for antisocial behavior. The famous Austrian psychologist Sigmund Freud* and his followers argued that individuals became radicalized because of traumas they suffered in their youth. Hoffer always maintained that they chose to join a radical organization in an attempt to compensate for feelings of inadequacy. Hoffer located the root cause of antisocial tendencies in people's feelings of worthlessness or self-hatred. He refused to accept the idea that it was something that people were not even conscious of that might explain someone's behavior and instead insisted that an individual's behavior stems from his or her own sense of self. This notion has been much more useful for social psychologists and terror scholars than searching for mysterious, unconscious thoughts.

### The Continuing Debate

As useful as *The True Believer* is in training counterterrorism units, it remains equally useful as a way to dismiss ideas you happen to disagree with. Hoffer argued that all mass movements stem from emotional reactions rather than ideology and he really did mean all mass movements, from fascists to Roman Catholics. Naturally, the Roman Catholics did not appreciate this but, after all, who enjoys having their ideas dismissed?

Hoffer's approach directly contrasts with that of many modern scholars who are trying to understand the "root causes" of terrorism. The University of Chicago political scientist Robert Pape* is just one person to have argued that we should not treat terrorism as the product of some kind of hatred or of a psychological lashing out. Rather, we should view it as terrorists undoubtedly do—as a mostly effective tactic for achieving certain political goals.[4]

Ironically, thinkers on both sides of the debate seem to have ignored a lot of the potential in the original text. Counterterrorism experts have refocused attention on Hoffer's insights about how mass movements cultivate extremism but ignore Hoffer's own emphasis on the sociological conditions that breed frustration and desperation in the first place. Scholars, meanwhile, most often cite *The True Believer* as proof that no one can reason with terrorists while ignoring the more nuanced approach where we might also read it as supporting the argument that the "root causes" of terrorism lie in difficult economic conditions and political stagnation. After all, radical leaders can only build a following by preying on the fear and discontent of marginalized populations. Therefore, if we could offer these marginalized, discontented people equal opportunities, it might be much harder for radical leaders to build a following.

## NOTES

1   Jerrold M. Post, "When Hatred is Bred in the Bone: Psycho cultural Foundations of Contemporary Terrorism." *Political Psychology* 26, no .4 (2005): 615–36.

2   Jerrold M. Post, *The Mind of the Terrorist: The Psychology of Terrorism from the IRA to al-Qaeda* (London: Palgrave Macmillan, 2007), 1.

3   Joe Navarro, *Hunting Terrorists: A Look at the Psychopathology of Terror*, 2nd edn (Springfield, IL: Charles C. Thomas Publisher, 2013), 30.

4   Robert Pape, *Dying to Win: The Strategic Logic of Suicide Terrorism* (New York: Random House, 2005).

# MODULE 12
# WHERE NEXT?

## KEY POINTS

- *The True Believer* has become a key text in the growing field of terrorism studies.

- Modern scholars of terrorism still build on the questions Hoffer first raised over 60 years ago in *The True Believer*.

- Today, Hoffer's ideas are used by police forces and academics alike.

### Potential

In *The True Believer*, Eric Hoffer offers very few thoughts about how to counteract the rise of mass movements.* Yet, people who study terrorism increasingly turn to his work for answers. Inspired by Hoffer, social psychologists* have compared a terrorist leader to "a malevolent group therapist who focuses the discontent of group members on an external cause for their difficulties."[1] Others mention Hoffer when discussing the importance of redirecting people's frustrations more productively. In effect, modern counterterrorist campaigns must act as the "men of words" Hoffer described. As one scholarly analysis put it, "The counter-terrorism agent must become adept at manipulating and transmitting messages which resonate among a population."[2]

Hoffer also continues to influence conservative* media figures. Leading American conservative political commentator Pat Buchanan* argued, "To understand the appeal to such men of ISIS,* despite its beheadings, crucifixions, slaughter of prisoners, rape and sale into slavery of the daughters and wives of enemies, there are few better sources than the longshoreman-philosopher Eric Hoffer."[3] Increasingly, these ideas have attracted conservative thought leaders in

> **❝** The follower or Idealist ... One of the best characterizations of this person was completed and published by a self educated writer, Eric Hoffer. **❞**
>
> Thomas Strentz, "A Terrorist Operational Profile"

other parts of the world. In 2015, Australia's foreign minister offered a lengthy review of Hoffer's text to explain why people join ISIS, the so-called Islamic State.[4]

### Future Directions

Will the problems Hoffer addressed ever be resolved? And if they are, how much will Hoffer's mid-twentieth-century analysis of mass movements contribute to the solution? *The True Believer* remains part of the curriculum the US Federal Bureau of Investigation* uses to train new counterterrorism agents and it has already provided the FBI* with critical insights in at least one investigation.[5] Declassified documents provide some insight into the ways Hoffer's theories shape modern security practices. In 2008, the FBI referenced Hoffer's work in a report on an American citizen who became the editor of an online magazine for al-Qaeda* in the Arabian Peninsula. An unidentified investigator reported to his superiors that, "In an attempt to understand why Samir Khan* has chosen the path that he is on, writer reviewed Eric Hoffer's *The True Believer*, which was written as a general overview of the nature of mass movements (not any one in particular)."[6] This is a fascinating insight, but because so many of these operations remain classified, we will likely not know the full impact Hoffer's work has had on US security policies for many years to come.

### Summary

Despite his unconventional educational background, Eric Hoffer has been shaping public policy in the United States for more than sixty years. In *The True Believer*, Hoffer concentrated on the psychological suffering of the people who join radical movements. He also addressed the ways mass movements shape those initial insecurities into fanatical hatred. The work articulates at least some of the reasons why people become willing to join groups that lie so far outside the mainstream. Today, Hoffer's text provides plenty of material for both liberal* and conservatives to develop their approaches to mass movements.

In the aftermath of World War II,* Hoffer's work fundamentally shaped public opinion about the Soviet Union.* His book fell out of favor in the second half of the twentieth century but after the al-Qaeda terror attacks on the United States on September 11, 2001* its insights into the nature of fringe movements seemed more relevant than ever. Hoffer wrote about the ways mass movements cultivate a "readiness to die" in the name of "fanaticism." In an era of suicide bombings, his work offers a powerful language for understanding the causes of people whose stated beliefs remain difficult to understand in what most of us might consider rational terms.

Regardless of the extent to which we can apply insights from *The True Believer* to today's extremist groups, the book continues to have a major impact on security policy. It is still essential reading not only for analysts of al-Qaeda and ISIS, but also for anyone who wants to understand the philosophy behind, and development of, counterterrorism policies in the United States. Of course it is also vital reading for those who implement those policies, and *The True Believer* will undoubtedly remain essential reading for a long, long time.

## NOTES

1   Jerrold M. Post, "When Hatred Is Bred in the Bone: Psycho-Cultural Foundations of Contemporary Terrorism," *Political Psychology* 26, no. 4 (2005): 618.

2   Keely M. Fahoum and Jon Width, "Marketing Terror: Effects of Anti-Messaging on GSPC Recruitment," *Strategic Insights* 5, no. 8 (2006), accessed October 22, 2015, http://oai.dtic.mil/oai/

oai?verb=getRecord&metadataPrefix=html&identifier=ADA521344.

3   Pat Buchanan, "Terrorism and the True Believer," *TribLive*, October
    28, 2014, accessed October 22, 2015, http://triblive.com/opinion/
    featuredcommentary/7041834-74/isis-devil-hoffer#axzz3pMKW2VPV.

4   Julie Bishop, "Battling the Orwellian nightmare of Islamic State's mind
    control," *Australian Financial Review*, March 18, 2015, accessed October
    22, 2015, http://www.afr.com/opinion/columnists/battling-the-orwellian-
    nightmare-of-islamic-states-mind-control-20150318-1m20p7.

5   Federal Bureau of Investigation, "Career Development Plan"
    (2010), accessed October 22, 2015, https://www.aclu.org/files/
    fbimappingfoia/20150309/ACLURM017011.pdf.

6   Jason Leopold, "The FBI Used a 1951 Book to Gain Insight into an American
    al Qaeda Subject," *VICE News*, February 4, 2015, accessed October 22,
    2015, https://news.vice.com/article/the-fbi-used-a-1951-book-to-gain-insight-
    into-an-american-al-qaeda-suspect.

# GLOSSARY

# GLOSSARY OF TERMS

**Al-Qaeda:** a global Islamic terrorist organization founded by Osama bin Laden. It is best known for carrying out the September 11, 2001 attacks in the United States, the 2002 bombings of nightclubs in Bali, and the 2005 bombings of London's transport system.

**American dream:** a characteristic belief in the United States that hard work and honesty will lead to social and economic advancement.

**American exceptionalism:** the idea that the United States remains fundamentally different from all other nations, because of its devotion to liberty, individualism, capitalism, and democracy.

**American Revolution (1765–83):** the political movement and war that overthrew British colonialism, resulting in the founding of the United States of America.

**Amorphous:** lacking any clear organizing principle, structure, or focus.

**Anomie:** a technical sociological term referring to the breakdown of social norms that guide individual behavior.

**Anti-Vietnam War movement:** one of the largest antiwar movements in the United States, it demanded that the US withdraw from the war it waged in Vietnam from 1964 through 1975.
**Asceticism:** a lifestyle characterized by the avoidance of indulgence, especially in worldly pleasures.

**Authoritarianism:** a form of government characterized by the absolute obedience to authority; regimes tend to be governed by autocratic "presidents for life," and deeply related to a cult of personality surrounding the leader.

**Black Lives Matter:** a twenty-first-century activist movement in the United States that was organized in response to police violence against African Americans.

**Capitalism:** an economic system based on private ownership, private enterprise, and the maximization of profit.

**Civil Rights Movement (1954–68):** an organized political effort to end legal discrimination against African Americans in the United States.

**Cold War (1946–89):** a period of tension between America and the Soviet Union. While the two countries never engaged in direct military conflict, they engaged in covert and proxy wars and espionage against one another.

**Colonialism:** a social, political, and economic phenomenon by which several European nations established control over nations in other parts of the world.

**Communism:** a political ideology that relies on the state ownership of the means of production, the collectivization of labor, and the abolition of social class.

**Conservatism:** a political philosophy that promotes a return to traditional moral values and the defense of existing institutions.

**Cult:** the usually pejorative term for a religious group, often small in numbers, that believes in religious ideals outside the mainstream.

**Democracy:** a form of government where citizens elect a body of representatives who will then act in their name.

**Disposition:** in psychology, a habit or tendency to act in a specific way.

**Dixiecrats:** a short-lived American political party dedicated to maintaining states' rights to segregation.

**Fascism:** an authoritarian, and usually dictatorial, form of right-wing government. Prominent examples include Nazi Germany and Benito Mussolini's Italy.

**Federal Bureau of Investigation (FBI):** the domestic intelligence, security, and federal law enforcement agency of the United States.

**Free Speech Movement:** a student movement in the United States between 1964 and 1965 that demanded the lifting of a ban on political activities on campuses, and acknowledgment of students' rights to free speech.

**French Renaissance:** part of the broader European "renaissance," or rebirth, this was a period of rapid cultural, technological, and philosophical innovation in France from the fifteenth to the seventeenth century. Historians have classically identified the rapid changes characteristic of the Renaissance period as the birth of the modern world.

**French Revolution (1789–99):** a period of massive political upheaval in France, during which rebels overthrew the monarchy and aristocracy. Scholars usually consider the French Revolution to be one of the most influential events of the modern era.

**Freudian psychoanalysis:** a method of analyzing psychological illnesses, which usually searches for the unconscious motivations of human actions.

**Hippies:** a subculture popular in the 1960s United States, characterized by free love, embracing diversity, and rock and roll music.**Humanist psychology:** a branch of psychology that believes all people are inherently good and works with people to realize their authentic selves.

**Impressionistic:** views or reactions that are presented randomly and that are based on a subjective approach.

**Indian independence movement (1920s–1947):** a political movement to gain India's independence from the British Empire. Although this anticolonial movement had both violent and nonviolent elements, the Indian independence movement became famous for the nonviolent civil disobedience tactics preached by its leaders, most notably Mohandas Karmachand "Mahatma" Gandhi.

**Individualism:** a moral philosophy emphasizing independence, self-reliance, and the realization of self-interest.

**ISIS:** the Islamic State of Iraq and the Levant, also known as IS, ISIL, or Daesh, is an Islamic terrorist group. It rose to prominence in the early 2010s by exerting effective control over large parts of Iraq and Syria.**Islam:** a monotheistic (belief in one God) religion based on the Qur'an. Its followers are known as Muslims.

**Islamic fundamentalism:** a modern and still controversial term designating a wide variety of conservative Islamic religious movements, including but not limited to certain terrorist groups.

**Korean War (1950–3):** a war between communist North Korea, supported by the Soviet Union, and democratic South Korea, supported by the United States.

**Liberalism:** a political philosophy that emphasizes freedom, equality, and regularly contested elections.

**Marxism:** an economic philosophy based on the writings of Karl Marx, which emphasized the importance of class struggle as the engine of history.

**Mass movements:** a popular term in the mid-twentieth century, mass movements referred to the politicization of new urban populations, usually in response to an emotional or irrational appeal. Today, we would use terms like "radical," "extremist," or "populist" to talk about groups that fall under this heading.

**Mohammedan:** antiquated term for a Muslim.

**National Commission on the Causes and Prevention of Violence (1968):** a US presidential commission set up after the assassinations of Senator Robert Kennedy and Civil Rights leader Dr. Martin Luther King Jr. to investigate the causes of violence and social unrest.

**Nationalist:** a person who expresses belief in the interests of their own nation-state as a priority.

**Nazism:** also known as National Socialism, Nazism is a form of fascism associated with the twentieth-century German state and characterized by virulent racism and anti-Semitism.

**Neo-Nazis:** the term for a variety of post-World War II political movements that seek to revive the ideas associated with Nazism.

**Occupy Wall Street:** a 2011 protest movement in the United States against growing economic inequality.

**Paradigm:** a set of concepts, methods, and ways of thoughts that define what counts as a legitimate contribution in a given scientific field.

**Populism:** a political doctrine that supports the interests of "the common people" against those of "the elite." Although it has not always carried negative connotations, in twentieth- and twenty-first-century America the term is most often associated with charismatic politicians who make impractical yet emotionally appealing overtures to voters.

**Presidential Medal of Freedom:** the highest civilian honor in the United States.

**Psychoanalysis:** the theories of the mind associated with Sigmund Freud and his followers, psychoanalysis emphasizes the importance of unconscious mental processes to a person's behavior and emotions.

**Puritanism:** a sixteenth- and seventeenth-century English Protestant movement that sought to purify the Church of England from Roman Catholic influences.

**Reformation:** a movement beginning in Europe in the early sixteenth century, and around 1517 by Martin Luther in Germany. The Reformation began as a result of disputes over the teachings and practices of the Roman Catholic Church, and a separated, reformed church emerged, the Protestant Church that still exists today.

**Russian Revolution (1917):** a revolutionary uprising that toppled the czarist autocracy and saw the beginnings of the Soviet Union.

**Scientific racism:** a pseudo-scientific practice that attempted to classify characteristics to certain races in order to prove the superiority or inferiority of different groups of people.

**Self-esteem:** a person's own evaluation of his or her value. This can be an evaluation of skills and beliefs, or an emotional assessment of themselves.

**September 11, 2001 attacks (9/11):** this date saw four significant attacks on the United States by al-Qaeda, a terrorist organization. The attacks resulted in nearly 3,000 deaths.

**Social psychology:** the study of how social context shapes an individual's thoughts, emotions, and behavior.

**Soviet Union (1922–91):** also known as the Union of Soviet Socialist Republics (USSR), the Soviet Union was a communist state and one of the protagonists of the Cold War.

**Spartan:** refers to the ancient Greek city-state of Sparta, whose residents famously practiced austerity and self-discipline. By way of analogy, Spartan is also used to describe any highly disciplined group.

**Stalinism:** the system of government implemented in the Soviet Union by Joseph Stalin, who adopted policies characterized by state terror, rapid industrialization, and a centralized state. **Tea Party movement:** a conservative twenty-first-century political movement in the United States, dedicated to reducing the size of government and fighting against mandated universal health care.

**Totalitarianism:** a political system in which the state seeks to regulate all aspects of its citizens' lives. Totalitarian states do not recognize any degree of individual liberty.

**World War II (1939–45):** a global war that pitted the Allied Powers, led by the United States, Britain, France, and the Soviet Union, against the Axis Powers, led by Nazi Germany. The war resulted in an estimated 50–85 million deaths. **Zionism:** a national political movement that seeks to establish a homeland for the Jewish people in Palestine/Israel.

**Zulu:** an indigenous people native to South Africa. In 1879, the Zulu nation fought a bloody war to protect their independence against colonial Britain.

# PEOPLE MENTIONED IN THE TEXT

**Tom Bethell (b. 1940)** is a conservative American journalist who has written a biography of Eric Hoffer, based in large part on Hoffer's personal journals.

**Nathaniel Branden (1930–2014)** was a Canadian American psychotherapist. He is best known for his writings on self-esteem.

**Patrick J. Buchanan (b. 1938)** is a conservative political commentator based in the United States and one of the co-founders of the magazine *The American Conservative.*

**Oliver Cromwell (1599–1658)** was an English military and political leader who became the Lord Protector of the Commonwealth of England, Scotland and Ireland from 1653 to 1658 following the English Civil War (1642–51). His rule was characterized by harsh repression of Catholics and his political opponents.

**Peter Drucker (1909–2005)** was an American consultant and business writer. In addition to writing about fascism, Drucker is best known for his advocacy of decentralized and simplified corporate structures.

**R. Palme Dutt (1896–1974)** was a British journalist and member of the Communist Party. He is best known for advancing the argument that fascism was the result of a decaying form of financial capitalism.

**Dwight D. Eisenhower (1890–1969)** was the 34th president of the United States, in office from 1953 to 1961. He also served as Supreme Commander of Allied Forces in Europe during World War II.

**Sigmund Freud (1856–1939)** is considered the father of psychoanalysis. His ideas about the formation of identity and trauma still guide modern psychologists.

**Eric Fromm (1900–80)** was a German psychologist associated with the Frankfurt School of Social Research. He is best known for his detailed critique of Sigmund Freud.

**Mohandas Karmachand "Mahatma" Gandhi (1869–1948)** was the leader of the Indian independence movement against British colonialism. He is best known as a pioneer of nonviolent resistance.

**A. James Gregor (b. 1929)** is a political scientist at the University of California, Berkeley. He is best known for his research on the ideologies of fascism.

**Georg Wilhelm Friedrich Hegel (1770–1831)** was one of the most influential philosophers of the Enlightenment. Hegel saw all human history as the unfolding of an ideal Spirit.

**Lyndon B. Johnson (1908–73)** was the 36th president of the United States, in office from 1963 to 1969. He is best known for and is known for his Great Society program, as well as for his part in the escalation of the Vietnam War.

**Robert F. Kennedy (1925–68)** was an American politician. During the presidency of his older brother, John F. Kennedy (1960–64), he served as US attorney general; after his brother's assassination he became a US senator. Robert Kennedy was himself assassinated while campaigning for the presidency.

**Samir Khan (1985–2011)** was a Pakistani American affiliated with al-Qaeda. He is best known for editing the online magazine *Inspire*, which sought to recruit new volunteers for the terrorist organization.

**Osama bin Laden (1957–2011)** was the leader of al-Qaeda, the terrorist organization behind numerous mass-casualty acts of terrorism, including 9/11, until his assassination in 2011 by the US Navy.

**Gustave Le Bon (1841–1931)** was a French psychologist and sociologist. He is best known for his work on the urban crowd.

**Vladimir Lenin (1870–1924)** was one of the leaders of the Russian Revolution. He served as the Soviet Union's first head of state from 1922 until his death in 1924.

**Abraham Lincoln (1809–65)** was the 16th president of the United States, in office from 1861 until his assassination in 1865. He is best known for his leadership during the American Civil War and for signing the Emancipation Proclamation, officially ending slavery in the United States.

**Timothy Madigan** is an associate professor of philosophy at St. John Fisher College in Rochester, New York. He is also a regular contributor to *Philosophy Now* magazine.

**Michel de Montaigne (1533–92)** was one of the most significant philosophers of the French Renaissance. Among other things, his writings are often considered a forerunner of modern psychology.

**Benito Mussolini (1883–1945)** ruled Italy as prime minister beginning in 1922 and as dictator from 1925 to 1943. He is best known as one of the founders of European fascism.

**Peter Nathan (b. 1935)** is a psychologist at the University of Iowa. Later in his life, he changed to administrative roles as the provost and later president of the University of Iowa.

**Joe Navarro (b. 1953)** is a former FBI agent and an American author specializing in security studies. In addition to his writings on terrorism, he is well known for his studies of body language.

**José Ortega y Gasset (1883–1955)** was a Spanish liberal philosopher and essayist. Although he wrote frequently about politics, he is best known for his philosophical analysis of the self as composed of both the mind and the world it interacts with.

**Robert Pape (b. 1960)** is an American political scientist teaching at the University of Chicago. An expert in international security topics, he has published studies on the logic that motivates terrorism.

**Talcott Parsons (1902–79)** was an American sociologist who taught at Harvard University. He is best known for his contributions to positivist approaches to the study of societies.

**Richard Pipes (b. 1923)** is a historian teaching at Harvard University. He is best known for his strong anti-communist views, which informed his writings on Russian history.

**Jerrold Post** is professor of psychiatry, political psychology, and international affairs at the George Washington University. He has written extensively on the psychology of political violence and terrorism.

**Ronald Reagan (1911–2004)** was the 40th president of the United

States, in office from 1981 to 1989. He is best known as a leading figure of the conservative movement.

**Wilhelm Reich (1897–1957)** was an Austrian psychoanalyst who worked with Sigmund Freud. In addition to writing about the origins of fascism, Reich is best known for his research into the connections between psychology and body movements.

**Franklin Delano Roosevelt (1882–1945)** was the 32nd and longest-serving president of the United States, in office from 1933 to 1945. He is best known for leading the country through World War II and for passing the New Deal, a series of social programs aimed at alleviating poverty brought about by the Great Depression.

**Bertrand Russell (1872–1970)** was a British philosopher and public intellectual. He is best known for developing the field of analytic philosophy.

**Arthur Schlesinger Jr. (1917–2007)** was a historian who taught at Harvard University. He is best known for his book on the history of American liberalism.

**Bernard Theall (d. 1982)** was a Benedictine monk and the editor of the Catholic Encyclopedia.

**Evan Thomas (1920–99)** was a senior editor for Harper & Brothers, famous for acquiring books that would achieve success. Born into a politically active family, Thomas was a self-professed socialist.

# WORKS CITED

# WORKS CITED

Arendt, Hannah. *The Origins of Totalitarianism.* New York: Schoken Books, 1951.

Bates, Rodger A. "Terrorism within the Community Context." *Journal of Public and Professional Sociology* 3, no. 1 (2010).

Bethell, Tom. *Eric Hoffer: The Longshoreman Philosopher.* Stanford, CA: Hoover Institution Press, 2012.

Bishop, Julie. "Battling the Orwellian nightmare of Islamic State's mind control." *Australian Financial Review,* March 18, 2015. Accessed October 22, 2015. http://www.afr.com/opinion/columnists/battling-the-orwellian-nightmare-of-islamic-states-mind-control-20150318-1m20p7.

Blumenthal, Max. "Ike's Other Warning." *New York Times,* September 2, 2009. Accessed October 22, 2015. http://www.nytimes.com/2009/09/03/opinion/03blumenthal.html.

"Books: Dockside Montaigne." *Time,* March 14, 1955. Accessed October 22, 2015. http://content.time.com/time/magazine/article/0,9171,807143,00.html.

Branden, Nathaniel. *The Six Pillars of Self Esteem.* New York: Random House, 1995.

Buchanan, Pat. "Terrorism and the True Believer." *TribLive,* October 28, 2014. Accessed October 22, 2015. http://triblive.com/opinion/featuredcommentary/7041834-74/isis-devil-hoffer#axzz3pMKW2VPV.

Cupp, S. E. "What Occupy Wall Street and the Tea Party have in common: Right or left, all mass movements are the same." *New York Daily News,* November 16, 2011. Accessed October 22, 2015. http://www.nydailynews.com/opinion/occupy-wall-street-tea-party-common-left-mass-movements-article-1.977949#ixzz2LRkultyc.

Drucker, Peter. *The End of Economic Man: The Origins of Totalitarianism.* New York: Harper & Row, 1969.

Dutt, Rajani Palme. *Fascism: An Analysis.* Allahabad: India Publishers, 1943.

Fahoum, Keely M., and Jon Width. "Marketing Terror: Effects of Anti-Messaging on GSPC Recruitment." *Strategic Insights* 5, no. 8 (2006). Accessed October 22, 2015. http://oai.dtic.mil/oai/oai?verb=getRecord&metadataPrefix=html&identifier=ADA521344.

Federal Bureau of Investigation. "Career Development Plan." 2010. Accessed October 22, 2015. https://www.aclu.org/files/fbimappingfoia/20150309/ACLURM017011.pdf.

Fromm, Eric. *Escape From Freedom*. New York: Holt Paperbacks, 2008.

Gregor, A. James. *Fascism: The Contemporary Interpretations*. Morristown, NJ: General Learning Corporation, 1973.

— — —. *Interpretations of Fascism.* Morristown, NJ: General Learning Press, 1974.

Grissman, Gene. "The Weariness of a True Believer: Eric Hoffer's Parting Words." *San Francisco Chronicle*, July 10, 1983.

Hoffer, Eric. *The True Believer: Thoughts on the Nature of Mass Movements.* New York: Harper & Row, 1951.

— — —. *In Our Time*. New York: Harper & Row, 1976.

— — —. *The Ordeal of Change*. New York: Buccaneer Books, 1976.

— — —. *The Temper of Our Time*. New York: Hopewell Publications, 1976.

— — —. *The Passionate State of Mind and Other Aphorisms.* New York: Hopewell Publications, 2006.

Iklé, Fred Charles. *How Nations Negotiate*. New York: Harper & Row, 1964.

Le Bon, Gustav. *The Crowd: A Study of the Popular Mind*. New York: Viking, 1960.

Leopold, Jason. "The FBI Used a 1951 Book to Gain Insight into an American al Qaeda Subject." *VICE News,* February 4, 2015. Accessed October 22, 2015. https://news.vice.com/article/the-fbi-used-a-1951-book-to-gain-insight-into-an-american-al-qaeda-suspect.

Madigan, Tim. "The True Believer Revisited." *Philosophy Now* 34. Accessed October 22, 2015. https://philosophynow.org/issues/34/The_True_Believer_Revisited.

Nathan, Peter. *The Psychology of Fascism.* New York: Faber, 1943.

Navarro, Joe. *Hunting Terrorists: A Look at the Psychopathology of Terror*. Second Edition. Springfield, IL: Charles C. Thomas Publisher, 2013.

Ortega y Gasset, José. *Revolt of the Masses*. New York: W. W. Norton and Co., 1993.

Pape, Robert. *Dying to Win: The Strategic Logic of Suicide Terrorism*. New York: Random House, 2005.

Parsons, Talcott. *Essays in Sociological Theory*. New York: Free Press, 1949.

Post, Jerrold M. "When Hatred Is Bred in the Bone: Psycho-Cultural Foundations of Contemporary Terrorism." *Political Psychology* 26, no. 4 (2005): 615–36.

— — —. *The Mind of the Terrorist: The Psychology of Terrorism from the IRA to al-Qaeda*. London: Palgrave Macmillan, 2007.

Reagan, Ronald, "Remarks at the Presentation Ceremony for the Presidential Medal of Freedom." Reagan Presidential Library, February 23, 1983. Accessed October 22, 2015. http://www.reagan.utexas.edu/archives/speeches/1983/22383c.htm.

Reich, Wilhelm. *The Mass Psychology of Fascism*. New York: Orgone Institute Press, 1946.

Sevareid, Eric. *The Passionate State of Mind*. CBS, broadcast September 17, 1967.

Shachtman, Tom. *American Iconoclast: The Life and Times of Eric Hoffer*. New York: Hopewell Publications, 2011.

Strentz, Thomas. "A Terrorist Operational Profile: A Psycho-Social Paradigm and Plan for Their Destruction." In *Understanding and Responding to the Terrorism Phenomenon: A Multi-Dimensional Perspective*, edited by O. Nikbay and S. Hancerli, 19–27. Fairfax, VA: IOS Press, 2007.

Theall, Bernard. "When Does a Believer Become a Fanatic?" *Books on Trial*, April 1951.

# THE MACAT LIBRARY
# BY DISCIPLINE

**AFRICANA STUDIES**

Chinua Achebe's *An Image of Africa: Racism in Conrad's Heart of Darkness*
W. E. B. Du Bois's *The Souls of Black Folk*
Zora Neale Huston's *Characteristics of Negro Expression*
Martin Luther King Jr's *Why We Can't Wait*
Toni Morrison's *Playing in the Dark: Whiteness in the American Literary Imagination*

**ANTHROPOLOGY**

Arjun Appadurai's *Modernity at Large: Cultural Dimensions of Globalisation*
Philippe Ariès's *Centuries of Childhood*
Franz Boas's *Race, Language and Culture*
Kim Chan & Renée Mauborgne's *Blue Ocean Strategy*
Jared Diamond's *Guns, Germs & Steel: the Fate of Human Societies*
Jared Diamond's *Collapse: How Societies Choose to Fail or Survive*
E. E. Evans-Pritchard's *Witchcraft, Oracles and Magic Among the Azande*
James Ferguson's *The Anti-Politics Machine*
Clifford Geertz's *The Interpretation of Cultures*
David Graeber's *Debt: the First 5000 Years*
Karen Ho's *Liquidated: An Ethnography of Wall Street*
Geert Hofstede's *Culture's Consequences: Comparing Values, Behaviors, Institutes and Organizations across Nations*
Claude Lévi-Strauss's *Structural Anthropology*
Jay Macleod's *Ain't No Makin' It: Aspirations and Attainment in a Low-Income Neighborhood*
Saba Mahmood's *The Politics of Piety: The Islamic Revival and the Feminist Subject*
Marcel Mauss's *The Gift*

**BUSINESS**

Jean Lave & Etienne Wenger's *Situated Learning*
Theodore Levitt's *Marketing Myopia*
Burton G. Malkiel's *A Random Walk Down Wall Street*
Douglas McGregor's *The Human Side of Enterprise*
Michael Porter's *Competitive Strategy: Creating and Sustaining Superior Performance*
John Kotter's *Leading Change*
C. K. Prahalad & Gary Hamel's *The Core Competence of the Corporation*

**CRIMINOLOGY**

Michelle Alexander's *The New Jim Crow: Mass Incarceration in the Age of Colorblindness*
Michael R. Gottfredson & Travis Hirschi's *A General Theory of Crime*
Richard Herrnstein & Charles A. Murray's *The Bell Curve: Intelligence and Class Structure in American Life*
Elizabeth Loftus's *Eyewitness Testimony*
Jay Macleod's *Ain't No Makin' It: Aspirations and Attainment in a Low-Income Neighborhood*
Philip Zimbardo's *The Lucifer Effect*

**ECONOMICS**

Janet Abu-Lughod's *Before European Hegemony*
Ha-Joon Chang's *Kicking Away the Ladder*
David Brion Davis's *The Problem of Slavery in the Age of Revolution*
Milton Friedman's *The Role of Monetary Policy*
Milton Friedman's *Capitalism and Freedom*
David Graeber's *Debt: the First 5000 Years*
Friedrich Hayek's *The Road to Serfdom*
Karen Ho's *Liquidated: An Ethnography of Wall Street*

John Maynard Keynes's *The General Theory of Employment, Interest and Money*
Charles P. Kindleberger's *Manias, Panics and Crashes*
Robert Lucas's *Why Doesn't Capital Flow from Rich to Poor Countries?*
Burton G. Malkiel's *A Random Walk Down Wall Street*
Thomas Robert Malthus's *An Essay on the Principle of Population*
Karl Marx's *Capital*
Thomas Piketty's *Capital in the Twenty-First Century*
Amartya Sen's *Development as Freedom*
Adam Smith's *The Wealth of Nations*
Nassim Nicholas Taleb's *The Black Swan: The Impact of the Highly Improbable*
Amos Tversky's & Daniel Kahneman's *Judgment under Uncertainty: Heuristics and Biases*
Mahbub Ul Haq's *Reflections on Human Development*
Max Weber's *The Protestant Ethic and the Spirit of Capitalism*

## FEMINISM AND GENDER STUDIES

Judith Butler's *Gender Trouble*
Simone De Beauvoir's *The Second Sex*
Michel Foucault's *History of Sexuality*
Betty Friedan's *The Feminine Mystique*
Saba Mahmood's *The Politics of Piety: The Islamic Revival and the Feminist Subject*
Joan Wallach Scott's *Gender and the Politics of History*
Mary Wollstonecraft's *A Vindication of the Rights of Woman*
Virginia Woolf's *A Room of One's Own*

## GEOGRAPHY

The Brundtland Report's *Our Common Future*
Rachel Carson's *Silent Spring*
Charles Darwin's *On the Origin of Species*
James Ferguson's *The Anti-Politics Machine*
Jane Jacobs's *The Death and Life of Great American Cities*
James Lovelock's *Gaia: A New Look at Life on Earth*
Amartya Sen's *Development as Freedom*
Mathis Wackernagel & William Rees's *Our Ecological Footprint*

## HISTORY

Janet Abu-Lughod's *Before European Hegemony*
Benedict Anderson's *Imagined Communities*
Bernard Bailyn's *The Ideological Origins of the American Revolution*
Hanna Batatu's *The Old Social Classes And The Revolutionary Movements Of Iraq*
Christopher Browning's *Ordinary Men: Reserve Police Batallion 101 and the Final Solution in Poland*
Edmund Burke's *Reflections on the Revolution in France*
William Cronon's *Nature's Metropolis: Chicago And The Great West*
Alfred W. Crosby's *The Columbian Exchange*
Hamid Dabashi's *Iran: A People Interrupted*
David Brion Davis's *The Problem of Slavery in the Age of Revolution*
Nathalie Zemon Davis's *The Return of Martin Guerre*
Jared Diamond's *Guns, Germs & Steel: the Fate of Human Societies*
Frank Dikotter's *Mao's Great Famine*
John W Dower's *War Without Mercy: Race And Power In The Pacific War*
W. E. B. Du Bois's *The Souls of Black Folk*
Richard J. Evans's *In Defence of History*
Lucien Febvre's *The Problem of Unbelief in the 16th Century*
Sheila Fitzpatrick's *Everyday Stalinism*

Eric Foner's *Reconstruction: America's Unfinished Revolution, 1863-1877*
Michel Foucault's *Discipline and Punish*
Michel Foucault's *History of Sexuality*
Francis Fukuyama's *The End of History and the Last Man*
John Lewis Gaddis's *We Now Know: Rethinking Cold War History*
Ernest Gellner's *Nations and Nationalism*
Eugene Genovese's *Roll, Jordan, Roll: The World the Slaves Made*
Carlo Ginzburg's *The Night Battles*
Daniel Goldhagen's *Hitler's Willing Executioners*
Jack Goldstone's *Revolution and Rebellion in the Early Modern World*
Antonio Gramsci's *The Prison Notebooks*
Alexander Hamilton, John Jay & James Madison's *The Federalist Papers*
Christopher Hill's *The World Turned Upside Down*
Carole Hillenbrand's *The Crusades: Islamic Perspectives*
Thomas Hobbes's *Leviathan*
Eric Hobsbawm's *The Age Of Revolution*
John A. Hobson's *Imperialism: A Study*
Albert Hourani's *History of the Arab Peoples*
Samuel P. Huntington's *The Clash of Civilizations and the Remaking of World Order*
C. L. R. James's *The Black Jacobins*
Tony Judt's *Postwar: A History of Europe Since 1945*
Ernst Kantorowicz's *The King's Two Bodies: A Study in Medieval Political Theology*
Paul Kennedy's *The Rise and Fall of the Great Powers*
Ian Kershaw's *The "Hitler Myth": Image and Reality in the Third Reich*
John Maynard Keynes's *The General Theory of Employment, Interest and Money*
Charles P. Kindleberger's *Manias, Panics and Crashes*
Martin Luther King Jr's *Why We Can't Wait*
Henry Kissinger's *World Order: Reflections on the Character of Nations and the Course of History*
Thomas Kuhn's *The Structure of Scientific Revolutions*
Georges Lefebvre's *The Coming of the French Revolution*
John Locke's *Two Treatises of Government*
Niccolò Machiavelli's *The Prince*
Thomas Robert Malthus's *An Essay on the Principle of Population*
Mahmood Mamdani's *Citizen and Subject: Contemporary Africa And The Legacy Of Late Colonialism*
Karl Marx's *Capital*
Stanley Milgram's *Obedience to Authority*
John Stuart Mill's *On Liberty*
Thomas Paine's *Common Sense*
Thomas Paine's *Rights of Man*
Geoffrey Parker's *Global Crisis: War, Climate Change and Catastrophe in the Seventeenth Century*
Jonathan Riley-Smith's *The First Crusade and the Idea of Crusading*
Jean-Jacques Rousseau's *The Social Contract*
Joan Wallach Scott's *Gender and the Politics of History*
Theda Skocpol's *States and Social Revolutions*
Adam Smith's *The Wealth of Nations*
Timothy Snyder's *Bloodlands: Europe Between Hitler and Stalin*
Sun Tzu's *The Art of War*
Keith Thomas's *Religion and the Decline of Magic*
Thucydides's *The History of the Peloponnesian War*
Frederick Jackson Turner's *The Significance of the Frontier in American History*
Odd Arne Westad's *The Global Cold War: Third World Interventions And The Making Of Our Times*

## LITERATURE

Chinua Achebe's *An Image of Africa: Racism in Conrad's Heart of Darkness*
Roland Barthes's *Mythologies*
Homi K. Bhabha's *The Location of Culture*
Judith Butler's *Gender Trouble*
Simone De Beauvoir's *The Second Sex*
Ferdinand De Saussure's *Course in General Linguistics*
T. S. Eliot's *The Sacred Wood: Essays on Poetry and Criticism*
Zora Neale Huston's *Characteristics of Negro Expression*
Toni Morrison's *Playing in the Dark: Whiteness in the American Literary Imagination*
Edward Said's *Orientalism*
Gayatri Chakravorty Spivak's *Can the Subaltern Speak?*
Mary Wollstonecraft's *A Vindication of the Rights of Women*
Virginia Woolf's *A Room of One's Own*

## PHILOSOPHY

Elizabeth Anscombe's *Modern Moral Philosophy*
Hannah Arendt's *The Human Condition*
Aristotle's *Metaphysics*
Aristotle's *Nicomachean Ethics*
Edmund Gettier's *Is Justified True Belief Knowledge?*
Georg Wilhelm Friedrich Hegel's *Phenomenology of Spirit*
David Hume's *Dialogues Concerning Natural Religion*
David Hume's *The Enquiry for Human Understanding*
Immanuel Kant's *Religion within the Boundaries of Mere Reason*
Immanuel Kant's *Critique of Pure Reason*
Søren Kierkegaard's *The Sickness Unto Death*
Søren Kierkegaard's *Fear and Trembling*
C. S. Lewis's *The Abolition of Man*
Alasdair MacIntyre's *After Virtue*
Marcus Aurelius's *Meditations*
Friedrich Nietzsche's *On the Genealogy of Morality*
Friedrich Nietzsche's *Beyond Good and Evil*
Plato's *Republic*
Plato's *Symposium*
Jean-Jacques Rousseau's *The Social Contract*
Gilbert Ryle's *The Concept of Mind*
Baruch Spinoza's *Ethics*
Sun Tzu's *The Art of War*
Ludwig Wittgenstein's *Philosophical Investigations*

## POLITICS

Benedict Anderson's *Imagined Communities*
Aristotle's *Politics*
Bernard Bailyn's *The Ideological Origins of the American Revolution*
Edmund Burke's *Reflections on the Revolution in France*
John C. Calhoun's *A Disquisition on Government*
Ha-Joon Chang's *Kicking Away the Ladder*
Hamid Dabashi's *Iran: A People Interrupted*
Hamid Dabashi's *Theology of Discontent: The Ideological Foundation of the Islamic Revolution in Iran*
Robert Dahl's *Democracy and its Critics*
Robert Dahl's *Who Governs?*
David Brion Davis's *The Problem of Slavery in the Age of Revolution*

Alexis De Tocqueville's *Democracy in America*
James Ferguson's *The Anti-Politics Machine*
Frank Dikotter's *Mao's Great Famine*
Sheila Fitzpatrick's *Everyday Stalinism*
Eric Foner's *Reconstruction: America's Unfinished Revolution, 1863-1877*
Milton Friedman's *Capitalism and Freedom*
Francis Fukuyama's *The End of History and the Last Man*
John Lewis Gaddis's *We Now Know: Rethinking Cold War History*
Ernest Gellner's *Nations and Nationalism*
David Graeber's *Debt: the First 5000 Years*
Antonio Gramsci's *The Prison Notebooks*
Alexander Hamilton, John Jay & James Madison's *The Federalist Papers*
Friedrich Hayek's *The Road to Serfdom*
Christopher Hill's *The World Turned Upside Down*
Thomas Hobbes's *Leviathan*
John A. Hobson's *Imperialism: A Study*
Samuel P. Huntington's *The Clash of Civilizations and the Remaking of World Order*
Tony Judt's *Postwar: A History of Europe Since 1945*
David C. Kang's *China Rising: Peace, Power and Order in East Asia*
Paul Kennedy's *The Rise and Fall of Great Powers*
Robert Keohane's *After Hegemony*
Martin Luther King Jr.'s *Why We Can't Wait*
Henry Kissinger's *World Order: Reflections on the Character of Nations and the Course of History*
John Locke's *Two Treatises of Government*
Niccolò Machiavelli's *The Prince*
Thomas Robert Malthus's *An Essay on the Principle of Population*
Mahmood Mamdani's *Citizen and Subject: Contemporary Africa And The Legacy Of Late Colonialism*
Karl Marx's *Capital*
John Stuart Mill's *On Liberty*
John Stuart Mill's *Utilitarianism*
Hans Morgenthau's *Politics Among Nations*
Thomas Paine's *Common Sense*
Thomas Paine's *Rights of Man*
Thomas Piketty's *Capital in the Twenty-First Century*
Robert D. Putman's *Bowling Alone*
John Rawls's *Theory of Justice*
Jean-Jacques Rousseau's *The Social Contract*
Theda Skocpol's *States and Social Revolutions*
Adam Smith's *The Wealth of Nations*
Sun Tzu's *The Art of War*
Henry David Thoreau's *Civil Disobedience*
Thucydides's *The History of the Peloponnesian War*
Kenneth Waltz's *Theory of International Politics*
Max Weber's *Politics as a Vocation*
Odd Arne Westad's *The Global Cold War: Third World Interventions And The Making Of Our Times*

## POSTCOLONIAL STUDIES

Roland Barthes's *Mythologies*
Frantz Fanon's *Black Skin, White Masks*
Homi K. Bhabha's *The Location of Culture*
Gustavo Gutiérrez's *A Theology of Liberation*
Edward Said's *Orientalism*
Gayatri Chakravorty Spivak's *Can the Subaltern Speak?*

## PSYCHOLOGY

Gordon Allport's *The Nature of Prejudice*
Alan Baddeley & Graham Hitch's *Aggression: A Social Learning Analysis*
Albert Bandura's *Aggression: A Social Learning Analysis*
Leon Festinger's *A Theory of Cognitive Dissonance*
Sigmund Freud's *The Interpretation of Dreams*
Betty Friedan's *The Feminine Mystique*
Michael R. Gottfredson & Travis Hirschi's *A General Theory of Crime*
Eric Hoffer's *The True Believer: Thoughts on the Nature of Mass Movements*
William James's *Principles of Psychology*
Elizabeth Loftus's *Eyewitness Testimony*
A. H. Maslow's *A Theory of Human Motivation*
Stanley Milgram's *Obedience to Authority*
Steven Pinker's *The Better Angels of Our Nature*
Oliver Sacks's *The Man Who Mistook His Wife For a Hat*
Richard Thaler & Cass Sunstein's *Nudge: Improving Decisions About Health, Wealth and Happiness*
Amos Tversky's *Judgment under Uncertainty: Heuristics and Biases*
Philip Zimbardo's *The Lucifer Effect*

## SCIENCE

Rachel Carson's *Silent Spring*
William Cronon's *Nature's Metropolis: Chicago And The Great West*
Alfred W. Crosby's *The Columbian Exchange*
Charles Darwin's *On the Origin of Species*
Richard Dawkin's *The Selfish Gene*
Thomas Kuhn's *The Structure of Scientific Revolutions*
Geoffrey Parker's *Global Crisis: War, Climate Change and Catastrophe in the Seventeenth Century*
Mathis Wackernagel & William Rees's *Our Ecological Footprint*

## SOCIOLOGY

Michelle Alexander's *The New Jim Crow: Mass Incarceration in the Age of Colorblindness*
Gordon Allport's *The Nature of Prejudice*
Albert Bandura's *Aggression: A Social Learning Analysis*
Hanna Batatu's *The Old Social Classes And The Revolutionary Movements Of Iraq*
Ha-Joon Chang's *Kicking Away the Ladder*
W. E. B. Du Bois's *The Souls of Black Folk*
Émile Durkheim's *On Suicide*
Frantz Fanon's *Black Skin, White Masks*
Frantz Fanon's *The Wretched of the Earth*
Eric Foner's *Reconstruction: America's Unfinished Revolution, 1863-1877*
Eugene Genovese's *Roll, Jordan, Roll: The World the Slaves Made*
Jack Goldstone's *Revolution and Rebellion in the Early Modern World*
Antonio Gramsci's *The Prison Notebooks*
Richard Herrnstein & Charles A Murray's *The Bell Curve: Intelligence and Class Structure in American Life*
Eric Hoffer's *The True Believer: Thoughts on the Nature of Mass Movements*
Jane Jacobs's *The Death and Life of Great American Cities*
Robert Lucas's *Why Doesn't Capital Flow from Rich to Poor Countries?*
Jay Macleod's *Ain't No Makin' It: Aspirations and Attainment in a Low Income Neighborhood*
Elaine May's *Homeward Bound: American Families in the Cold War Era*
Douglas McGregor's *The Human Side of Enterprise*
C. Wright Mills's *The Sociological Imagination*

Thomas Piketty's *Capital in the Twenty-First Century*
Robert D. Putman's *Bowling Alone*
David Riesman's *The Lonely Crowd: A Study of the Changing American Character*
Edward Said's *Orientalism*
Joan Wallach Scott's *Gender and the Politics of History*
Theda Skocpol's *States and Social Revolutions*
Max Weber's *The Protestant Ethic and the Spirit of Capitalism*

## THEOLOGY

Augustine's *Confessions*
Benedict's *Rule of St Benedict*
Gustavo Gutiérrez's *A Theology of Liberation*
Carole Hillenbrand's *The Crusades: Islamic Perspectives*
David Hume's *Dialogues Concerning Natural Religion*
Immanuel Kant's *Religion within the Boundaries of Mere Reason*
Ernst Kantorowicz's *The King's Two Bodies: A Study in Medieval Political Theology*
Søren Kierkegaard's *The Sickness Unto Death*
C. S. Lewis's *The Abolition of Man*
Saba Mahmood's *The Politics of Piety: The Islamic Revival and the Feminist Subject*
Baruch Spinoza's *Ethics*
Keith Thomas's *Religion and the Decline of Magic*

## COMING SOON

Chris Argyris's *The Individual and the Organisation*
Seyla Benhabib's *The Rights of Others*
Walter Benjamin's *The Work Of Art in the Age of Mechanical Reproduction*
John Berger's *Ways of Seeing*
Pierre Bourdieu's *Outline of a Theory of Practice*
Mary Douglas's *Purity and Danger*
Roland Dworkin's *Taking Rights Seriously*
James G. March's *Exploration and Exploitation in Organisational Learning*
Ikujiro Nonaka's *A Dynamic Theory of Organizational Knowledge Creation*
Griselda Pollock's *Vision and Difference*
Amartya Sen's *Inequality Re-Examined*
Susan Sontag's *On Photography*
Yasser Tabbaa's *The Transformation of Islamic Art*
Ludwig von Mises's *Theory of Money and Credit*

The Macat Library By Discipline

# Macat Disciplines

*Access the greatest ideas and thinkers across entire disciplines, including*

## *Postcolonial Studies*

**Roland Barthes's** *Mythologies*
**Frantz Fanon's** *Black Skin, White Masks*
**Homi K. Bhabha's** *The Location of Culture*
**Gustavo Gutiérrez's** *A Theology of Liberation*
**Edward Said's** *Orientalism*
**Gayatri Chakravorty Spivak's** *Can the Subaltern Speak?*

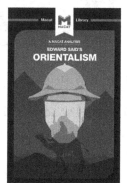

Macat analyses are available from all good bookshops and libraries.

Access hundreds of analyses through one, multimedia tool.
Join free for one month **library.macat.com**

# Macat Disciplines

*Access the greatest ideas and thinkers across entire disciplines, including*

## AFRICANA STUDIES

**Chinua Achebe's** *An Image of Africa: Racism in Conrad's Heart of Darkness*

**W. E. B. Du Bois's** *The Souls of Black Folk*

**Zora Neale Hurston's** *Characteristics of Negro Expression*

**Martin Luther King Jr.'s** *Why We Can't Wait*

**Toni Morrison's** *Playing in the Dark: Whiteness in the American Literary Imagination*

Macat analyses are available from all good bookshops and libraries.

Access hundreds of analyses through one, multimedia tool.
Join free for one month **library.macat.com**

# Macat Disciplines

*Access the greatest ideas and thinkers across entire disciplines, including*

## FEMINISM, GENDER AND QUEER STUDIES

**Simone De Beauvoir's**
*The Second Sex*

**Michel Foucault's**
*History of Sexuality*

**Betty Friedan's**
*The Feminine Mystique*

**Saba Mahmood's**
*The Politics of Piety:
The Islamic Revival and
the Feminist Subject*

**Joan Wallach Scott's**
*Gender and the
Politics of History*

**Mary Wollstonecraft's**
*A Vindication of the
Rights of Woman*

**Virginia Woolf's**
*A Room of One's Own*

**Judith Butler's**
*Gender Trouble*

Macat analyses are available from all good bookshops and libraries.

Access hundreds of analyses through one, multimedia tool.
Join free for one month **library.macat.com**

# Macat Disciplines

*Access the greatest ideas and thinkers across entire disciplines, including*

## CRIMINOLOGY

**Michelle Alexander's**
*The New Jim Crow: Mass Incarceration in the Age of Colorblindness*

**Michael R. Gottfredson & Travis Hirschi's**
*A General Theory of Crime*

**Elizabeth Loftus's**
*Eyewitness Testimony*

**Richard Herrnstein & Charles A. Murray's**
*The Bell Curve: Intelligence and Class Structure in American Life*

**Jay Macleod's**
*Ain't No Makin' It: Aspirations and Attainment in a Low-Income Neighborhood*

**Philip Zimbardo's**
*The Lucifer Effect*

Macat analyses are available from all good bookshops and libraries.

Access hundreds of analyses through one, multimedia tool.
Join free for one month **library.macat.com**

# Macat Disciplines

*Access the greatest ideas and thinkers across entire disciplines, including*

## INEQUALITY

**Ha-Joon Chang's,** *Kicking Away the Ladder*

**David Graeber's,** *Debt: The First 5000 Years*

**Robert E. Lucas's,** *Why Doesn't Capital Flow from Rich To Poor Countries?*

**Thomas Piketty's,** *Capital in the Twenty-First Century*

**Amartya Sen's,** *Inequality Re-Examined*

**Mahbub Ul Haq's,** *Reflections on Human Development*

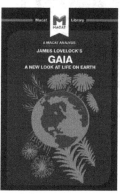

# Macat Disciplines

*Access the greatest ideas and thinkers across entire disciplines, including*

## *THE FUTURE OF DEMOCRACY*

**Robert A. Dahl's,** *Democracy and Its Critics*
**Robert A. Dahl's,** *Who Governs?*
**Alexis De Toqueville's,** *Democracy in America*
**Niccolò Machiavelli's,** *The Prince*
**John Stuart Mill's,** *On Liberty*
**Robert D. Putnam's,** *Bowling Alone*
**Jean-Jacques Rousseau's,** *The Social Contract*
**Henry David Thoreau's,** *Civil Disobedience*

# Macat Disciplines

*Access the greatest ideas and thinkers across entire disciplines, including*

## TOTALITARIANISM

**Sheila Fitzpatrick's,** *Everyday Stalinism*
**Ian Kershaw's,** *The "Hitler Myth"*
**Timothy Snyder's,** *Bloodlands*

# Macat Pairs

*Analyse historical and modern issues from opposite sides of an argument. Pairs include:*

## RACE AND IDENTITY

### Zora Neale Hurston's
*Characteristics of Negro Expression*

Using material collected on anthropological expeditions to the South, Zora Neale Hurston explains how expression in African American culture in the early twentieth century departs from the art of white America. At the time, African American art was often criticized for copying white culture. For Hurston, this criticism misunderstood how art works. European tradition views art as something fixed. But Hurston describes a creative process that is alive, ever-changing, and largely improvisational. She maintains that African American art works through a process called 'mimicry'—where an imitated object or verbal pattern, for example, is reshaped and altered until it becomes something new, novel—and worthy of attention.

### Frantz Fanon's
*Black Skin, White Masks*

*Black Skin, White Masks* offers a radical analysis of the psychological effects of colonization on the colonized.

Fanon witnessed the effects of colonization first hand both in his birthplace, Martinique, and again later in life when he worked as a psychiatrist in another French colony, Algeria. His text is uncompromising in form and argument. He dissects the dehumanizing effects of colonialism, arguing that it destroys the native sense of identity, forcing people to adapt to an alien set of values—including a core belief that they are inferior. This results in deep psychological trauma.

Fanon's work played a pivotal role in the civil rights movements of the 1960s.

Macat analyses are available from all good bookshops and libraries.

Access hundreds of analyses through one, multimedia tool.
Join free for one month **library.macat.com**

# Macat Pairs

*Analyse historical and modern issues from opposite sides of an argument. Pairs include:*

## *INTERNATIONAL RELATIONS IN THE 21ST CENTURY*

### Samuel P. Huntington's
*The Clash of Civilisations*

In his highly influential 1996 book, Huntington offers a vision of a post-Cold War world in which conflict takes place not between competing ideologies but between cultures. The worst clash, he argues, will be between the Islamic world and the West: the West's arrogance and belief that its culture is a "gift" to the world will come into conflict with Islam's obstinacy and concern that its culture is under attack from a morally decadent "other."

Clash inspired much debate between different political schools of thought. But its greatest impact came in helping define American foreign policy in the wake of the 2001 terrorist attacks in New York and Washington.

### Francis Fukuyama's
*The End of History and the Last Man*

Published in 1992, *The End of History and the Last Man* argues that capitalist democracy is the final destination for all societies. Fukuyama believed democracy triumphed during the Cold War because it lacks the "fundamental contradictions" inherent in communism and satisfies our yearning for freedom and equality. Democracy therefore marks the endpoint in the evolution of ideology, and so the "end of history." There will still be "events," but no fundamental change in ideology.

# Macat Pairs

*Analyse historical and modern issues from opposite sides of an argument. Pairs include:*

## HOW TO RUN AN ECONOMY

### John Maynard Keynes's
*The General Theory OF Employment, Interest and Money*

Classical economics suggests that market economies are self-correcting in times of recession or depression, and tend toward full employment and output. But English economist John Maynard Keynes disagrees.

In his ground-breaking 1936 study *The General Theory*, Keynes argues that traditional economics has misunderstood the causes of unemployment. Employment is not determined by the price of labor; it is directly linked to demand. Keynes believes market economies are by nature unstable, and so require government intervention. Spurred on by the social catastrophe of the Great Depression of the 1930s, he sets out to revolutionize the way the world thinks

### Milton Friedman's
*The Role of Monetary Policy*

Friedman's 1968 paper changed the course of economic theory. In just 17 pages, he demolished existing theory and outlined an effective alternate monetary policy designed to secure 'high employment, stable prices and rapid growth.'

Friedman demonstrated that monetary policy plays a vital role in broader economic stability and argued that economists got their monetary policy wrong in the 1950s and 1960s by misunderstanding the relationship between inflation and unemployment. Previous generations of economists had believed that governments could permanently decrease unemployment by permitting inflation—and vice versa. Friedman's most original contribution was to show that this supposed trade-off is an illusion that only works in the short term.

Macat analyses are available from all good bookshops and libraries.

Access hundreds of analyses through one, multimedia tool.
Join free for one month **library.macat.com**

# Macat Pairs

*Analyse historical and modern issues from opposite sides of an argument. Pairs include:*

## HOW WE RELATE TO EACH OTHER AND SOCIETY

### Jean-Jacques Rousseau's
*The Social Contract*

Rousseau's famous work sets out the radical concept of the 'social contract': a give-and-take relationship between individual freedom and social order.

If people are free to do as they like, governed only by their own sense of justice, they are also vulnerable to chaos and violence. To avoid this, Rousseau proposes, they should agree to give up some freedom to benefit from the protection of social and political organization. But this deal is only just if societies are led by the collective needs and desires of the people, and able to control the private interests of individuals. For Rousseau, the only legitimate form of government is rule by the people.

### Robert D. Putnam's
*Bowling Alone*

In *Bowling Alone*, Robert Putnam argues that Americans have become disconnected from one another and from the institutions of their common life, and investigates the consequences of this change.

Looking at a range of indicators, from membership in formal organizations to the number of invitations being extended to informal dinner parties, Putnam demonstrates that Americans are interacting less and creating less "social capital" – with potentially disastrous implications for their society.

It would be difficult to overstate the impact of *Bowling Alone*, one of the most frequently cited social science publications of the last half-century.

Macat analyses are available from all good bookshops and libraries.

Access hundreds of analyses through one, multimedia tool.
Join free for one month **library.macat.com**

Printed in the United States
by Baker & Taylor Publisher Services